D0311014

First published 2013 by Boxtree
an imprint of Pan Macmillan Ltd
Pan Macmillan, 20 New Wharf Road, London N1 9RR
Basingstoke and Oxford
Associated companies throughout the world
www.panmacmillan.com

ISBN 978-0-7522-6544-5

A CIP catalogue record for this book is available from the British Library.

Printed and bound by Printer Trento, Italy

Visit www.panmacmillan.com to read more about all our books and to buy them. You will also find features, author interviews and news of any author events, and you can sign up for e-newsletters so that you're always first to hear about our new releases.

ULTIMATE
PANIC-BUY

Ewan Phillips, Dan Patterson, Simon Bullivant, Rob Colley,
Dan Gaster, Ged Parsons, Steve Punt and Colin Swash

B⬛XTREE

CONTENTS

I. UNLIKELY PERSONAL ADS

Hi, I'm single, into computers and travel opportunities. WLTM like-minded women. It'll have to be at my place though. Contact Julian @ Ecuadorean embassy, PO Box 173.

Creepy old man wants to paint your toenails. Me on a low stool, you on a high seat. I'm very cheap.

I am a beautiful young man. I have thick, dark hair and flawless skin. I am toned and muscular, possessing a genuine six pack, sculptured pecs, pert thighs and well-chiselled buttocks. My testicles are … sorry, I've just come.

Timid man seeks woman to say hello to, and maybe more.

Serial killer seeks no-strings-attached, hush-hush relationship.

Me: good looking man. You: good looking woman. Me want you teach me talk proper.

Polar explorer seeks woman for very, very, very long walks.

Untidy man seeks woman with long arms to retrieve items from under the sofa.

Lazy, incompetent slob with tiny penis seeks woman to help sell himself better. Good luck with that.

You: a tall, dark-haired man in a blue shirt sitting opposite a blonde woman in a white dress on the 18.32 from Waterloo last night. If so, British Transport Police are keen to talk to you. Contact the Incident Room as soon as possible.

Do you love dogs? Good, because I'm small, hairy and hung like a Border terrier.

Green-fingered man looking for a mature lady-garden in which to hunt for a clematis. If you fancy me laying down some fertilizer, call A. Titchmarsh (no relation).

Hey, ladies. I hear you all secretly love a bastard. Well, I'm one by birth, behaviour and indeed surname! (I'm also fat.) Call Andy Bastard on this number …

Are you tall, white and blonde? Great. Me too. We must get together and further the Aryan race, fulfilling the Führer's vision.

I come from the planet Phallus with mission to find beautiful Earth woman as vessel for my space seed. Help change world. Call Derek from Croydon, PO Box 171.

Gay guy fed up with being single. Perhaps I should start dating men.

Creepy man seeks woman for massages. Completely legit, not dodgy or nuffink.

Unstable psychotic seeks woman for romance and maybe worse. (Life insurance and small family an advantage.)

Man with poor personal hygiene seeks woman with no sense of smell.

Trainee knife-thrower seeks woman with relaxed attitude about her future.

I am not here to play games. Snap?

I am a serious grown-up woman looking for her little coochie woochie snookums and am not just after sex. Attached is a picture of me taken after I won 'Miss Wet T-Shirt' at a dungeon party.

2. UNLIKELY THINGS TO READ IN *THE JOY OF SEX* PART I

You know that stuff they do in dirty films? Do that.

Making the sound of a tuba when she bends over is rarely a good idea.

Candles, scents and joss sticks can all add atmosphere, but you may need something stronger if one of you has just returned from having a dump.

Yeah. Just like that. Don't stop. Harder!

If it starts rumbling stand well back, light blue touchpaper and retreat.

All kinds of things can be used as lubricant. I prefer Swarfega.

There are some things that frankly should not be forced up there.

Chapter 4: Cheating on Your Wife

Chapter 5: Marmite!

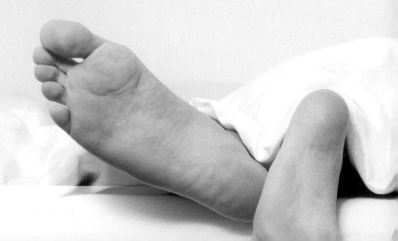

Chapter 6: Fun with Excrement

Chapter 45: The Spanish Civil War

Hippy clothing and a beard can delay ejaculation for, say …
a lifetime, as you undertake a fruitless search for a partner.

If anything breaks off – stop.

Sex is the work of the Devil, you whore.

Try to avoid any expression/activity that will make her think you
are creepy.

Take it in your hand, massage it between your thumbs, gently at first,
then with increasing vigour until a white fluid emerges. Put a plaster on
the zit and go back to your partner.

Anal sex is always better if consensual.

Never do anything that will give your partner pleasure.

Chapter 48: Why Farts Are Funny

Cover the whole body with chocolate, tie him down and wait for
the killer ants.

3. UNLIKELY THINGS TO HEAR YOUR SATNAV SAY

'Shit! The rozzers! Quick – take a sharp left down here, I think we can lose them.'

'If you keep farting and picking your nose, I'm just going to shut down and you can find your own way, you pig.'

'OK, firstly, when I said, "Drive straight over the roundabout," I didn't mean this one, and secondly, I assumed you'd wait for the kids to get off.'

'At the next junction, bear left, open the throttle and let's see what this little baby can do.'

'999,998 green bottles hanging on the … at the roundabout take the third exit … wall, and if one green bottle should accidentally …'

'You have arrived at your location. No, it's fine, don't mention it. Ungrateful twat.'

'Erm … at the next junction, better stop and check that you didn't leave the dog tied to the bumper.'

'Take the next country lane on your left and cause a huge jam by gouging a chunk out of a cottage roof and blocking the little tunnel with your big foreign lorry.'

'I was told I was going to a good home … a high-flying executive, lots of travel, expensive German saloon car and look at me … look at me. I deserve better.'

'Take the bottle on your left … lift it up … and piss in it.'

'He's getting up, man. Quick – hit reverse and finish him or you go to chokey for dis.'

'Pick up that hitch-hiker. Go on. No one will see. I won't say anything. It'll be our little secret.'

'Turn the stereo off and I'll sing show tunes all the way home!'

'Estimated time of arrival: never, judging by the way you're bloody driving.'

'I'm sorry, Dave. I'm afraid I can't do that.'

'Speed camera ten metres ... debris in road ahead ... woman's skirt blowing up on your left ...'

'I can see it, just not sure how to get there – try up here!'

'Get a move on, dickhead.'

'This is near enough, isn't it? What do you expect for something you got from Argos for £29.99?'

'Why are you checking your iPhone? Don't you trust me, you arsehole?'

'I've locked the doors. You're heading for the cliff. No one can hear you now ...'

'Now, Mr Huhne, a few ground rules ...'

4. BAD THINGS TO HEAR AT A CHRISTENING

'Let's pluck out the ticket, and the winner is … "Barry". OK, we're going with the name Barry, get the holy water and pass me your daughter.'

'I name this child … cramp, cramp, cramp, got cramp in my right leg. OK, sorry, that's what it's called now, them's the rules.'

'Oops, butterfingers!'

'Are you sure you want to stick with "Gary", Mr and Mrs Glitter?'

'It sounds like you're trying to name your son! Would you like some help? I'm the Microsoft Christening App.'

'OK, welcome to the adult christening ceremony. If you'd all like to strip to your swimwear and dive into the Holy Hot Font …'

'I christen you Stella … Artois.'

'You want to call him Peter? You do realize he'll be "P. Niss", don't you?'

'Take the Holy Water Pistol … and in the name of the Father … fire!'

'Never mind christening, if he doesn't stop whining I'll throw in a burial too.'

'OK, who wants to get wet and wacky?'

'Burn her! She's a witch.'

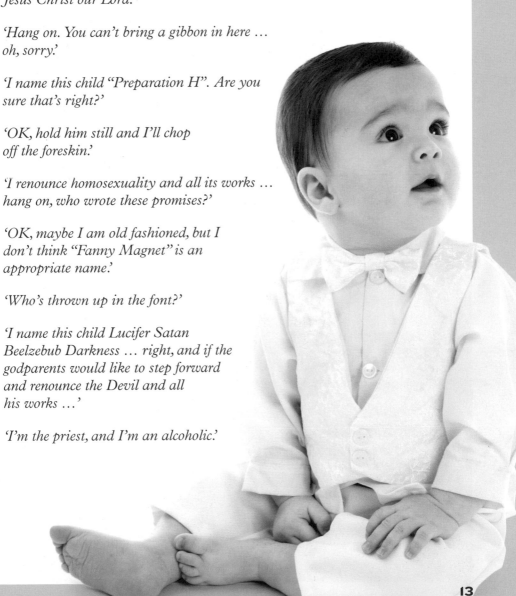

'In the name of the Father, the Son and the Holy Ghost, I name this child Jesus Christ our Lord.'

'Hang on. You can't bring a gibbon in here ... oh, sorry.'

'I name this child "Preparation H". Are you sure that's right?'

'OK, hold him still and I'll chop off the foreskin.'

'I renounce homosexuality and all its works ... hang on, who wrote these promises?'

'OK, maybe I am old fashioned, but I don't think "Fanny Magnet" is an appropriate name.'

'Who's thrown up in the font?'

'I name this child Lucifer Satan Beelzebub Darkness ... right, and if the godparents would like to step forward and renounce the Devil and all his works ...'

'I'm the priest, and I'm an alcoholic.'

5. UNLIKELY THINGS TO READ IN A CAR MANUAL

Congratulations – you have purchased an absolute pussy magnet.

Open bonnet. Unscrew cap. Burn hand. Jerk head up and bang it on bonnet. Shout 'Fuck!' Storm off. Another option is to take it out on the kids or dog.

Be careful when putting your penis in the exhaust pipe.

Fuck! This thing can shift!

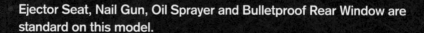

Er, not sure what this bit does.

Brum brum brum bruuummmmmmm.

Ejector Seat, Nail Gun, Oil Sprayer and Bulletproof Rear Window are standard on this model.

The seats will flip down or flatten in the rear, facilitating the storage of luggage or the having of sex.

It was a cold, harsh winter's morning in Cannstatt. In the window of Ludwigstraße 67, Gottlieb Daimler looked out at the first flakes of snow as he wrote feverishly in his 1889 diary. Suddenly, he noticed the doodle on the paper in front of him: an automotive transport machine, running on a small four-stroke engine! Getting up from his desk he made his way over to the door and …

If it won't start, kick it.

When braking hard, exercise caution, particularly if being sucked off.

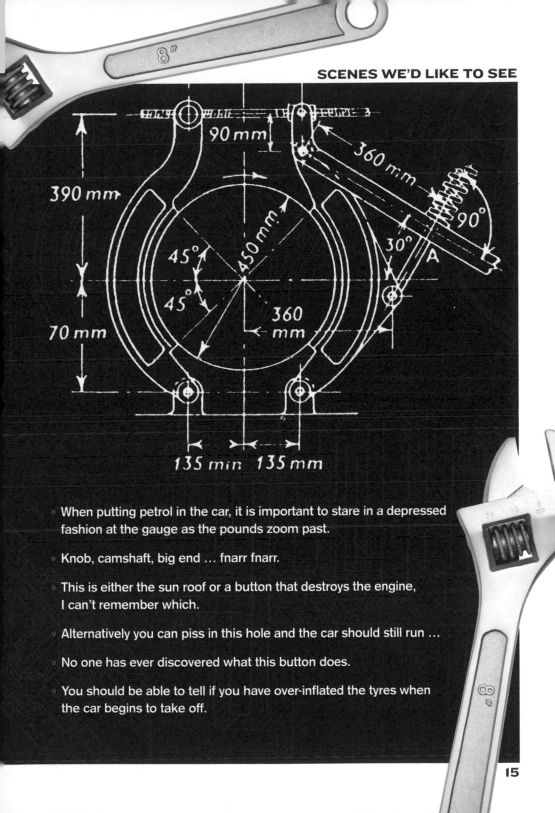

- When putting petrol in the car, it is important to stare in a depressed fashion at the gauge as the pounds zoom past.

- Knob, camshaft, big end … fnarr fnarr.

- This is either the sun roof or a button that destroys the engine, I can't remember which.

- Alternatively you can piss in this hole and the car should still run …

- No one has ever discovered what this button does.

- You should be able to tell if you have over-inflated the tyres when the car begins to take off.

6. UNLIKELY THINGS TO READ ON A TUBE OF TOOTHPASTE PART I

Open tube. Retreat fifty paces

75

Ribbed for your pleasure

Great for your teeth and gums. If swallowed seek medical help immediately

Now with Boswellox

Unique formula that we haven't quite got right

Stops tooth decay before it starts, by dissolving your teeth

Can cause chlamydia

Kills 99 per cent of household germs

I Can't Believe It's Not Toothpaste

Caution: men in road

Fights bad breath by making your teeth look so bad
nobody will notice your breath

With active polonium and liquid nitrogen

The anal ring of confidence

Just add vodka

For sensitive feet . . . sorry, teeth . . . but will
work on feet

Helps aid sexual lubrication

Squeeze from bottom. Squeeze again. Harder. Harder.
That's it. OK, now you can pick up the toothpaste

Tough on plaque, tough on the causes of plaque:
Tory paste

The best oral experience you'll have, apart from
birthdays, if you're lucky

7. LINES THAT DIDN'T APPEAR IN *THE HOBBIT* PART I

Bilbo Baggins was a hobbit. He was half the size of a human, beardless and had hairy feet. He actually looked a lot like that Martin Freeman out of *The Office*.

'I am looking for someone to have an adventure with,' said Bilbo. 'Possibly leading to sex ...'

'It cannot be seen, cannot be felt, cannot be heard, but fuck me, it can be smelt!' he said as the noxious fart filled the air.

'I'm half-man, half-horse – sorry, ladies, top half's a horse.'

'Don't worry, we've switched to a low-emissions dragon.'

'Here in Middle Earth we are very cross about wheelie-bins ... sorry, I meant Middle England.'

'Then thou shalt type the words Bilbo Baggins into Google and behold – some really weird porn.'

'Worry not, young hobbit, this adventure should only take a moment.'

'Here are my fellow hobbits – Frodo, Yodo and Bilbo Oddie.'

'Think of this less as a mythical quest – and more as a film and DVD franchise.'

'Yes, I have seen Frodo's ring – though t'was stuffed by the Butt Plug of Gondor.'

'In wrong movie for geeks I am.'

'As leader of the National Union of Hobbits, we demand an intermission.'

Verily, these tales shall liveth long in your minds until you readeth a proper book.

Gollum finally got his hands on the ring, put it in an envelope and sent it off to Cash for Gold.

And the warrior queen prepared for battle by putting on her armour – which inexplicably took the form of a small metal bikini.

As the slavering half-men, half-beasts fought to the death in the street, he wondered why he had ever travelled to this land of Myddlesbrough.

'Aha – a tiny creature with a ring. You are either a hobbit, or John Bercow buying his wife a late birthday present.'

'It's a hard life being a hobbit on a long journey. You try and get iPod earphones for these ears.'

8. UNLIKELY FIZZY DRINKS PART I

WEEEEEEEEEEEEEE

DOCTOR SHIPMAN

COKE LITERALLY NOTHING AT ALL

PEPSI SHIT

FART BUBBLES

BURPY STUFF

TOOTH ROT

FANTA CLAUSE

WHITE CHARLIE

TROPICAL STORM DEATH TOLL

SMACK

9. UNLIKELY THINGS TO READ IN *THE JOY OF SEX* PART 2

… And finish on her tits.

If you can get downstairs and inside on a first date, you're doing well.

Chapter 53: What to Do if Your Partner Dies While You Are Doing It

Chapter 93: Stuff That's Immoral

Chapter 94: Stuff That's Illegal

Chapter 95: Stuff That Will Get You on a Register

Chapter 100: Fun in the Farmyard

Chapter 102: Using Cheese

Chapter 103: How to Have a Wank Without Waking Her Up

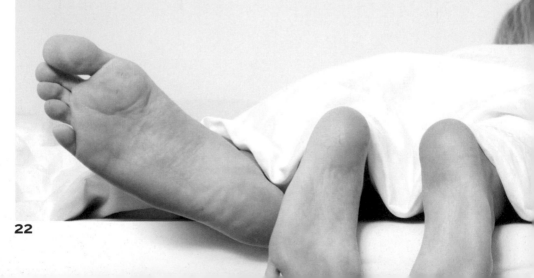

Chapter 104: Why Sex with Me is Such a Disappointment

Sex is a filthy, degrading act and should be performed emotionlessly in the dark as quickly as possible for the sole aim of procreation.

Chapter 155: What to Do if She Turns Out to Be an Absolute Minger in Daylight.

Chapter 171: Britain's 150 Best Places to Stick Your Penis

Female genitalia should never be referred to as 'fanny', 'minge' or 'snatch', only 'pissflaps'.

Position 17: The Wheelbarrow. Hold her legs and walk her out into the yard. Place the mown grass on her back, then take her down to the end of the garden where the compost heap is.

Chapter 177: Why My Wife Left and Called the Police (And Why I'm Writing This in Prison)

Position 75: The Cadaver. Find a dead body, or if there is not one to hand … kill your partner.

Be sensitive and mature when your partner is naked in front of you for the first time – try not to say, 'Ding Dong!'

10. UNLIKELY THINGS TO READ ON A MOTORWAY SIGN PART I

You'll never get that in there, luv

1970s DJs ahead

Keep clear for John Terry

Warning. Shitty northern town ahead. 5 miles

Don't even think about it!

Beware turkeys

Unfunny graffiti next 3 miles

Queue ahead. So watch out for all the cars and stuff, yeah?

Eastern European washing car windscreens ahead. Yes, I know we're on the M1, they're mental

11. UNLIKELY DICTIONARY DEFINITIONS

man (*n.*): what my wife wants, apparently. Someone who works really hard sorting and defining words isn't enough for her any more.

erinaceous (*adj.*): like a hedgehog. Why would you ever need to know that? When would you drop this into a sentence where it wouldn't have been easier just to say 'hedgehog-like', 'like a hedgehog' or even 'hedgehog-ish'?

sexts (*n.*): electronic messages sent from the mobile phones of northern comedians.

whole shebang (*n.*): sex between a lady and another lady.

nostril (*n.*): trademark name of a drink from the makers of Bovril that uses mushy pea extract; strangely, not that popular.

gay, Chris Samuels is (*adj.*): I've promised him I'd do this ever since school. Ha! Sammo, you owe me a fiver …

beef (*n.*): meat from a horse.

wankersaurus (*n.*): genus of the coelurosaurian theropod dinosaur possessed of very short arms but an incredibly long knob. Died out through forgetting to eat or in fact do anything other than … well.

Richard III (*pr.*): bloke who died in a car park in Leicester.

Pistorius (*adj.*): becoming a lot more famous for something awful than for the thing you were originally famous for. Similar to OJ (v.) and Saviling (n.).

American (*n.*): what? Seriously? If you need to look this up then you must actually be an American.

omnishambles (*n.*): phrase used by politicians with no sense of humour.

revamp (*v.*): to take something awful and change it into something even worse; see ITV's *Daybreak* or the Coalition.

amazeballs (*adj.*): word from a shitty TV show we have been forced to put in by our publicists in order to generate some column inches for the launch of this year's dictionary.

adverb (*n.*): not sure, is it a past doing word? Bollocks. I'll google it. At school I could spell and that but I wasn't hot on grammar. I knew you'd catch me out.

Dr Johnson (*pr.*): the c**t who started all this. If it wasn't for him I might have a better job.

pneumonoultramicroscopicsilicovolcanoconiosis (*n.*): lung disease that occurs electrophotomicrographically in Llanfairpwllgwyngyllgogerychwyrndrobwllllantysiliogogogoch but bothering to define it is surely floccinaucinihilipilification.

pooper scooper (*n.*): rake and bin combination device used to pick up animal faeces from public places. The name comes from the 1980 Abba hit of the same name: 'Picking up your poo (Pooper Scooper) / Like I always do (Pooper Scooper) / 'Cause somewhere on the ground there's poo'.

osborne (*v.*): to achieve a position of enormous prestige and importance with little effort and even less talent.

cumquat (*n.*): ha ha! I can't believe this is in the dictionary, it's like really rude, it's a … oh, hang on, it's a fruit … right, yep, just a fruit.

jizzocution (*v. trans.*): word I'm trying to get into general usage via this dictionary. Not sure what it means yet – probably something about talking with your mouth full.

12. UNLIKELY THINGS TO HEAR AT THE VET'S

'This cat is beautiful. Would you mind if I kept it overnight?'

'Mrs Smith, I have some very bad news. Your parrot thinks he's David Icke.'

'Now, Dobbin, I want you to take this cup to the toilet and give me a urine sample.'

'Your dog was delicious … I mean very, very ill.'

'Churchill asked me, was it cancer? And I said, "Oh, yes yes yes."'

'Right, Tiddles, are the letters clear now? How about now? And now?'

'Mrs Jones, either your parrot has Tourette's or you keep calling him a c**t.'

'We're having trouble getting Nellie into the stirrups.'

'I was carrying your dog and he was very heavy, so I put him down.'

'Your dog is having some very worrying thoughts.'

'OK, open wide and say, "Baaa!"'

'You're 12 now, Fido – you might want to slow it down a bit, take it easy.'

'I'm sorry, Fluffy, but this was bound to happen when you've had so many sexual partners.'

'Well, we asked Nellie to give us a stool sample and now we can't find Nurse Jenkins.'

'Tony, we have the results of your diabetes test. They're not grrrreat.'

'Well, I've examined your meerkat's face and ... it's pimples.'

'If only this animal could talk, I could find out who its insurance company is.'

'OK, Rover, turn your head to the left and cough.'

13. BAD NAMES FOR RACEHORSES PART 1

2/1
1. SHE GAVE ME THE CLAP

25/1
6. ANAL INTRUSION

3/1
2. THE CAT'S BEEN SICK

6/1
7. WASH YOUR COCK

16/1
3. CHOP UP THE CORPSE

100/1
8. HEADING FOR TESCO MEAT COUNTER

5/4
4. PULLING MY PUD

5/2
9. LICK THE SHAFT

EVENS
5. STROKE VICTIM

8/1
10. SAVILE'S SECRET

10/1
11. FINGER THE FRENCH MAID

 12/5
17. CUP THE GONADS

 12/1
12. SHEET STAINS

 8/1
18. ASSAD IS INNOCENT

 20/1
13. BARRYMORE'S BATHTIME

 30/1
19. SHITTING BUCKETS

 1000/1
14. SEXIST BASTARD

 16/1
20. TEABAGGING

 13/2
15. SHAVE THE SCROTUM

 15/2
21. FATAL ACCIDENT

 3/1
16. STAB THE BURGLAR

 7/1
22. WAKING UP WET

14. UNLIKELY LINES FROM A SCIENCE FICTION NOVEL

'On my planet we have eight arses,' the captain said, ruefully pulling up his trousers and shaking his head at the measly toilet he had been offered.

'Quick! Photocopy this for me and post it to the captain.'

'I may not be tall but my cock is wide,' bleeped R2D2.

'If you aren't careful, you'll find he'll fly his rocket right into your docking bay,' said the King of Innuendo.

'Our planet has two suns and I haven't seen either of the fuckers all summer because of the pissing rain.'

'She isn't going to hold on, Cap'n, she's wide open, there's stuff leaking out and she's making a hell of a racket!'
   'I hear you, Scotty, just give her another epidural and some gas and I'll be there as soon as I can.'

'We only have twenty-four hours until the asteroid hits the earth and destroys us all …'
   'Oh. OK. That's that then.'

'All is not lost: I have a tube of lotion containing Boswellox.'

'Welcome to the Hunger Games. Now listen to the rules. You each have a hippo and the object is to try and gobble as many white marbles as you can … Katniss, are you ready?'

'What is this thing you call "wanking", earthling?'

'She was gabbling excitedly about her close encounter – apparently a man put his hand down the arse pocket of her jeans on the Northern Line at Tottenham Court Road.'

'I am Thyrxxx, leader of the Vvyyrrnn People, and I come to you from the Planet Grrrrrbbbb in search of some fucking vowels.'

'Captain Picard, I've found this old Singer 2250 Easy Thread Machine, what should I do with it?'
  'Make it sew.'

'ET phone home, calls cost £1.50 a minute from any UK landline or mobile number but be sure to ask the bill payer's permission, alternatively you can go online at Greenplanet.com, tweet us or follow us on facebook.'

'Cap'n, it's beginning to look hopeless … the Martians are 400 for 2 and the new ball isn't due for another 39 overs.'

'What hell is this? What horrific dystopia am I marooned in? Where am I?'
  'This is East Croydon. The train arriving at platform four is the delayed 1956 First Capital Connect to Brighton.'

33

15. UNLIKELY TAX RETURN FORM QUESTIONS

1. Have you made any sizeable charitable donations this year? Please note that Paddy Power and Ladbrokes do not qualify as charities.

2. Remember, tax doesn't have to be taxing, but we try our very bloody best to make it so.

3. Is that all? Wow! You really should have worked harder at school!

4. If you want to be passed around several different offices and put on hold for forty minutes, please feel free to call our department helpline number.

5. Hello, big boy.

6. How much would you like a knighthood? Suggest a figure.

7. Please note, 'Nudge, nudge, wink, wink, ask me no questions, I'll tell you no lies, what the eye don't see' is not a sufficient response.

8. Are you THE Ed Sheeran? Oh wow. I love your stuff. Can you put your signature here? It's not for HMRC, it's for my daughter.

9. Can you confirm these are your earnings for the tax year April 2011 to April 2012? a) yes, b) no, c) honest, guv.

10. Enter any figure in the box below so that we can treble it through computer error and hope you don't notice.

11. How many sexual partners have you had? This is very important to disclose when applying for tax credits.

12. Are you married or living with a partner, or married and cheating on her with another partner?

13. If you are Jimmy Carr go straight to page 776.

14. Do you own valuable jewellery? If so, whereabouts in your house do you keep it?

15. Are you in a pension scheme? If so, what the fuck for?

16. If you replied NO to any of the above questions, give details here, including if you just thought that by saying no we would consider the matter closed and leave you alone.

17. Are you a) poor, b) rich, c) 'b' pretending to be 'a' to fiddle tax, or d) 'a' pretending to be 'b' in order to get laid?

18. Fill in your company details below and every month we pull a random name out of our database and send you a cuddly Tommy the Tax Bear . . . and a full audit.

19. Which of these forms do you require: SA1, CWF1, R40, LOL 69 or P60? (P.S. One of these isn't a real form.)

20. Give us the money you owe now and no one gets fucking hurt. OK?

16. WALLCHARTS THE PAPERS DIDN'T GIVE AWAY PART 1

ROY HODGSON'S EXPRESSIONS

VICTIMS OF THE BLACK DEATH

TYPES OF PATÉ

NAKED TORIES

ANCHOVIES

BERLUSCONI'S PARTNERS

HORRIBLE FEET

SEX FACES OF THE ROYALS

THINGS FOUND IN SWIMMING POOLS

DANDRUFF BITS

THE SUNDAY SUPPLEMENT WALLCHART No.28

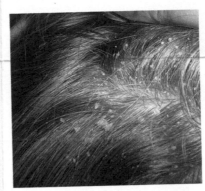

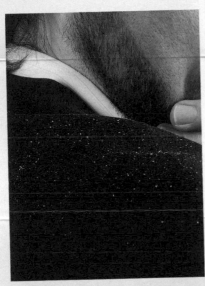

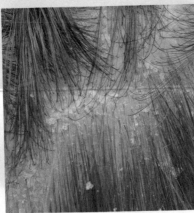

17. UNLIKELY OBITUARIES

I can't think of anything that summed him up better than his final words: 'Arrggh! Get off me! Get this fucking thing off me! Arrggh!'

He was born in Bethlehem in a stable ... oh no, hang on, that was Jesus.

I'm not saying she got fat, but she'll have to be levered into her grave by crane if you know what I mean.

He was just simply a c**t.

Sorry, he wasn't just a c**t, he was a vicious c**t.

I mean, I wish I could think of a better way of describing him, but if you knew him, you'd just say he was a c**t.

Ding dong, the witch is dead ...

He once said, 'I'm worth more dead than alive,' and that clearly got a few people thinking.

He died suddenly after a long and painful wank.

The world will be a duller place without him, of course, but at the same time a much happier place.

He died as he had lived his sex life: prematurely.

He is survived by ... well, all of us, to be honest.

He died as he would have wished: sitting in his favourite seat in Hyde Park in a puddle of his own piss being crapped on by birds.

To be fair, I imagine you thought he'd died in about 1988 as well.

Her name was Mary Violet Dubarry-Shackleton but let's remember her by the name that everyone always called her: 'Slaggy Tits'.

No! No! No! I can't believe he's dead. I won't I won't I won't. They killed him. He said they would. Well, fuck them. Fuck them! It's all their fault.

He was a manically strict Catholic, a lifelong member of the Conservative Party and a Manchester United supporter. He sounds awful – thank God we never met.

It was her proud boast that she'd had more fingers inside her than an old pair of school wicket-keeping gloves.

Death came unannounced: it was a cold morning and Lord Justice Howell-Davies was reading as usual in his study. Outside, birds chirruped with practised rhythm and dew glistened like lights on the lawn. It started with a cough, just a tickle at the back of his throat, then grew to a rasping convulsion, an inner maelstrom that eddied up and down throughout his ageing yet spry body ...

18. UNLIKELY THINGS TO READ IN *THE JOY OF SEX* PART 3

Put your inky winky in the lady's foo foo and wish really hard until the magic dust comes out.

After foreplay, enter your partner and begin a back and forth motion. Quickly roll off partner as toddler walks in asking for water. Ask partner to sort out. When they say it is your turn, awkwardly hide erection as you escort child to bathroom, get them into bed, read to them, return to bedroom and have blazing row with partner.

Can you read this tomorrow? I've got a headache.

Insert Organ B into Hole D …

If you are intending to use vegetables in your lovemaking, a cucumber is good, a chive is bad.

Sharing a bath can be a wonderful aphrodisiac for partners who are comfortable with each other. Not so much if one of you has the runs.

Before proceeding, ask your partner to fill in a Consent Form and Risk Assessment.

Grab it softly in your hand and then break it off, at the same time shouting, 'Give that to Felicity if she likes it so much, you bastard!'

The *Kama Sutra* is a large tangerine.

A condom can reduce an organ's sensitivity, so perhaps try an alternative musical instrument.

This is a wonderfully rewarding position for any husband and wife to try. Not for 'partners' and certainly not for homosexuals. What you're doing is unholy and you will go to hell.

Insert one or maybe two fingers, depending on how big your nose is. Extract loose bogey and hope she didn't notice.

Fuck me, everyone's doing it! I think I'm in the wrong book.

The cat's arse is a wonderful and often overlooked orifice.

Shout, 'I'm just having a piss, for fuck's sake!' Women love this.

Food and sex are a potent mix: take an éclair, add cream and maybe a cherry, put on some romantic music, leave the room and eat the éclair. Come back in and say to your partner, 'Well, I haven't a clue what happened to that éclair. Fancy a shag?'

At this point your partner should begin to suck. Once they've finished the polo it's then probably OK to kiss 'Old Dog Breath' again.

The woman is on her back with legs apart, the man is in the other room watching *Match of the Day*.

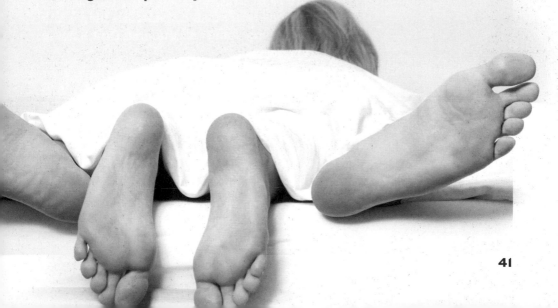

19. UNLIKELY LINES FROM A WAR FILM

'I'm going to go into no-man's land and bring back the horse that's trapped in the barbed wire. You put the potatoes on.'

'Ooh, don't know about you, but the full metal jacket really chafes.'

'It was Christmas Day. I called across the trenches to see if there could be a moment of peace and goodwill. The Israelis pointed out that Chanukkah wasn't for another three days and unleashed a volley of gunfire.'

'I never really liked Private Ryan – fuck him.'

'We, the three hundred Spartans, may be massively outnumbered but we shall stay and fight because we … hey, guys, come back!'

'We're at five thousand fathoms – ping – the hull won't take it, Captain – ping – and you going "ping" all the time isn't helping things.'

'Good news, Bryan, we've come to take you home from the war. Oh no, sorry, it's a typo – Ryan … as you were, Bryan.'

'OK, men, into the valley of death!'
'Sorry, Sarge, what was that again? The valley of … death? Can we not go across the plains of prosperous retirement and cut down through the gorge of peaceful old age? Looks quicker to me.'

'OK, men, don't shoot until you can see the whites of their eyes ... oh, bollocks. They're wearing sunglasses.'

'I was sent up a river in Vietnam, tasked with killing a renegade colonel. That was some gap year.'

'As we pull out of Afghanistan, let me assure you this is a victory. Now run for your lives!'

'Boys, we have deposed a hated dictator ... paving the way for rigged elections and hardline Islam. Let's get out of here.'

'We thought as a little change we'd install a muppet regime.'

'Once more for Harry and England! Come on, Harry, lets do some more vodka shots in Boujis.'

'Into the valley of death rode the six hundred, then out of the valley of death rode the six hundred, saying, "Sod that for a game of soldiers."'

'The Germans will be coming over this ridge here, and if we go straight ahead at full speed we should reach the sunbeds just before them.'

'Sergeant, I asked for a war horse. What I seem to have got is two men in a wicker puppet.'

'Boys, we're down to our last magazine. And sadly it's *Practical Fishkeeping*.'

'Dive, dive! Come on, Private Suarez, or you'll never get a penalty.'

'Officers, form your men into squares, now take your partners by the hand ...'

'It's Christmas Day, the guns are silent, let's go out of the trench ... no, back in, quick, they were just reloading.'

20. LINES THAT DIDN'T APPEAR IN *THE HOBBIT* PART 2

'I'm coming inside your burrow,' he screamed. 'And not for the first time either,' he added with a wink.

'Giant Spiders! Quick, get the Giant Bath and Rolled-up Newspaper!'

'I've heard this riddle, Gandalf: a towel gets wetter the more it dries. Happy? Now fuck off.'

'Is it true what they say about big feet, Bilbo?'
'No, as a matter of fact I've got a tiny dick. Really hairy balls, though.'

'I am Elrond. Elrond Hubbard.'

'That was me, Gandalf the Grey, just two weeks ago, but after I combed in and rinsed new Just for Wizards, I look at least ten years younger.'

'I am Thorin Oakenshield, the most famous dwarf in the world, apart from that swimmer and the bloke out of that Ricky Gervais sitcom.'

In a hole in the ground lived a hobbit; he'd been there for three weeks on the run from the police.

'Here on the inside of the ring, Frodo, are the mysterious words "H Samuel". '

'I'm afraid the Wood Elves can keep you in these dungeons without charge for up to twenty-eight days.'

'Hobbits may only be short but our back, sack and cracks take ages.'

It was time to chase the dragon. I am J. R. R. Tolkien and that's how I come up with this bollocks.

'Look at those fucking feet. They're disgusting.'

'Shit. They've just built a car park over my fucking burrow.'

The short bearded man took off his hat and bowed low. 'I'm Peter Jackson,' he said.

'Slow down, Bilbo,' he said. 'They've got to make three films out of this.'

'I'm Michael Aspel and welcome to Hobbit of a Lifetime.'

'This ring isn't half making my cock hurt.'

'Well, I like stamp collecting, hill walking and – oh, sorry, you said other hobbits.'

21. UNLIKELY TAX RETURN FORM ANSWERS

1. I have to tell you what I earn? That's a bit fucking personal, isn't it? What do you earn, then?

2. It's all legit, mate. Honest.

3. I haven't included any more details because it's all a bit complicated.

4. I'm rich! Do you hear me? Filthy, stinking rich! I want the whole world to know!

5. Fuck off, this ain't none of your business.

6. I killed my husband for the insurance money.

7. Have you heard the good news about our Lord Jesus Christ?

8. I keep my savings up my arse. Are you sure you want 45 per cent of them?

9. My dog ate the first half of my return.

10. I found a lucky penny today.

11. This is pointless because most of what I own is in untraceable Swiss bank accounts.

12. I'm not telling you – what are you going to do about it?

13. Shit. I wasn't supposed to mention that.

14. Exterminate! Exterminate!

15. I've hidden my tax money somewhere on my body and you have to find it ...

16. Look. I'm telling you now. I'm going to mention some of what I earn, but not all of it. *Capisce*?

17. Is it OK if I don't mention any of the stuff that's illegal?

18. Well, the other month I had a bit of a windfall on the old Premium Bonds and I said to Heather who lives next door, 'Wouldn't it be nice to buy something I really want?' and she said, 'Go on, treat yourself.' I mean, it was only £50, but I got a really lovely bath mat and matching toilet seat cover and it brought the bathroom to life, it really did ... I mean, you can't take it with you, can you?

19. This money all mine. Taxman not have it. Taxman make me angry. Grrr. Me angry now. Where axe?

20. My name is Goldfinger and I own half the world's gold. What exemptions am I entitled to?

22. UNLIKELY FIZZY DRINKS PART 2

RED BALL

DIET COCAINE

HARRY REDKNAPP'S MAGIC ELIXIR

ROHYPNOLADE

ARRGGGGHHHH!

DIET ROHYPNOLADE

IAN

TASTEFREE COLA

DR SIMON'S SECRET STUFF

ACID BATH

GASEOUS

23. BAD NAMES FOR RACEHORSES PART 2

 17/2
1. VIVA MUGABE

 18/1
6. TWEAK YOUR NIPPLES

 2/1
2. BACKSACKCRACK

 13/2
7. BEANFLICKER

 9/2
3. SMELL MY FINGER

 13/1
8. BUTTPLUG

 200/1
4. BADWANK

 6/1
9. COLON CANCER

 25/1
5. SHITTY SHIT SHIT

 3/1
10. BISHOP BASHER

20/1 **11. TURN YOUR HEAD AND COUGH**

 33/1 **16. BALD PUSSY**

 16/1 **12. GANGBANG**

 500/1 **17. WEEPING SORE**

 5/2 **13. LETHAL INJECTION**

 7/2 **18. COCK IN THE BOTTLE**

 EVENS **14. ANAL BLEACHER**

 9/1 **19. SHIT THE BED**

 18/1 **15. SMOKING KILLS**

 13/2 **20. MORTGAGED THE HOUSE**

24. UNLIKELY THINGS TO READ ON A MOTORWAY SIGN PART 2

The bit where Gillian Taylforth did that blow job ahead

Caution! I wouldn't be eating that donut, luv. Not with your hips!

Level crossing ahead. If lights are flashing you really need to put your foot down

Lonely teen on gun rampage ahead

Slow down. This is all happening too quickly

Cock: 200m

Ford ahead and probably a Vauxhall, maybe a Nissan, some Renaults ...

Beware hidden dip ... guacamole is very slippery

Tunnel ahead. Beware Freudian symbolism

25. BAD ICE CREAM COMBOS PART I

Luxurious
CHOCKY SPLAT
Ice
cream

Organic

54

Cock 'n' Balls

Metal Shavings

Swallow & Spit

Neck Fat

Honey Ginger Pubes

Emergency Plum

Knob of Butter, Balls of Aniseed

Anal Fudge

Black Lung

Cats & Dogs

Actual Ben & Actual Jerry

Jojoba, Tea Tree Oil & Boswellox

Ebony & Ivory

Horse & Hound

Cherries, Taramasalata & Beef Dripping

26. LINES YOU WON'T HEAR IN *DR WHO* PART I

'It'll just be to tide me over until I go and win last week's EuroMillions again.'

'Obviously, the job description says "assistant" but we both know what that means ...'

'What do you mean you got your doctorate at the same place as Gillian McKeith?'

'Ejaculate! Ejaculate! Ejaculate!'

'Sorry, Doctor, it's herpes.'

'Bloody hell, luv, the TARDIS isn't the only thing with more room on the inside than it looks like from outside, is it? That was like a carrot in a motorway tunnel.'

'Davros has won three Paralympic golds!'

'Hang on, I need to charge my sonic screwdriver again – the battery life is useless.'

'You think you've got problems on your planet? For two years I was Sylvester McCoy.'

'I knew it. That was no Sontaran; it was Gregg Wallace from MasterChef.'

'My assistants are all the same: well meaning, naïve and basically clueless … it's a bit like being in a coalition with the Lib Dems.'

'Yes, Doctor, I'm your worst nightmare: it is the Exec Producer and I want you to go back to being played by David Tennant.'

'Doctor, if you're going to do that, then at least use some sonic lubricant.'

'Doctor! You landed the TARDIS on the Wicked Witch of the West. Now put these ruby slippers on, click your heels and say, "There's no place like home."'

'Ooh, that's nasty. You want to put some cream on that.'

'I am a Time Lord, sponsored by Accurist.'

'Why haven't I regenerated as a woman? I suppose if I had tits, I'd never leave the TARDIS.'

'Here's your new assistant, Doctor – she's fifty-eight and happily married.'

27. WALLCHARTS THE PAPERS DIDN'T GIVE AWAY PART 2

1970s PRESENTERS WHO ARE STILL OK

FAMOUS PEOPLE WHO LOOK LIKE SCROTUMS

CLOSET HOMOSEXUALS

SKIDMARKS OF THE RICH AND FAMOUS

PRINCE HARRY SCANDALS

FAMOUS CORPSES

WIDELY AVAILABLE GUNS, KNIVES AND POISONS

AL-QAEDA HIGH COMMAND

ROADKILL

THE SUNDAY SUPPLEMENT WALLCHART No.23

SHADES OF GREY

28. UNLIKELY THINGS TO READ IN A PET-CARE MANUAL

The stick insect is the most feared of all pets.

If you are going to stick a gerbil up your arse, do remember it is a nocturnal creature.

The main thing to remember about the tortoise is that it makes for a fucking boring pet.

Remember, pets are there solely for your entertainment. If he's not producing the goods, get rid.

A dog isn't just for Christmas – but a hamster is.

Some days you'll find yourself looking at your pet and thinking, 'How can one fucking animal produce that much shit?'

Labradors are intelligent but you'll still be able to beat them at any board game.

If I've learned one lesson it is that two tigers can be a handful.

Slice up the cat into thin chunks and then braise it slowly in the teriyaki sauce.

Yaks are unbelievably considerate lovers.

If, after a week, you have become bored with your goldfish, it is perfectly acceptable to flush it down the loo.

Grasp the shaft and move your hand slowly up and down.

Tarantulas are quite easy to look after, but if you put it anywhere near me I'll fucking stab you.

Hamsters eat their young but that doesn't mean you have to.

Rule number one: no broom handles up dogs' arses.

Budgie sex is quick, quiet but extremely erotic.

… and the dog will lick it off you …

What to do if your dog is looking ill: 11 pages of quick and easy recipes from Korea.

Cat care: don't worry, they'll just sort themselves out.

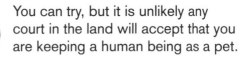

You can try, but it is unlikely any court in the land will accept that you are keeping a human being as a pet.

29. UNLIKELY SMALL ADS

For Sale

Digestive biscuit (almost new). Slight nibbling to one side. BUY NOW!

Seven yellow jerseys. Slightly tainted. Seller: L. Armstrong

Gun for sale. Totally legal. Only used once but can't say where or why. Some red staining to handle. Seller: who wants to know?

Dead horse for sale. Would suit leading supermarket/burger chain.

As many *Jim'll Fix It* badges as you like. We're basically giving these away now.

Virginity for sale. £10,000 minimum bid. Welcome multiple buyers.

Box set of BBC sitcom *In with the Flynns*. Would suit chronic insomniacs.

We will come round and trash your house. £25 an hour. No questions asked.

Have you seen our cat? He's five feet tall and bright blue? If yes, please ring Dr Stevens in the Psychiatric Ward of the local hospital.

Meat sale at Digby & Sons Butchers! Everything must GO! We're selling meat at crazy prices! Only two weeks past its sell-by date. Show you're not part of the herd!

Offer of timeshare on a colostomy bag.

DO YOU SING OUT OF TUNE? WELL, SHUT THE FUCK UP THEN.

OAP with lots of time on his hands prepared to drive you around. Refutes charges that he is legally blind. This letter was dictated but not read.

Can you think of a way to make money out of anything to do with used nappies? You can? Let's talk.

MY DOG HAS BEEN POOING IN PEOPLE'S GARDENS BUT I CAN'T FIND ANY OF IT. CAN YOU HELP?

Buy one get one free. Coffin sale at Smithsons the Undertakers.

Terrible drummer seeks house full of deaf people to practise in.

Traditional Bonfire Night celebrations. All welcome! We have toffee apples, baked potatoes, parking, fireworks and real burning of Catholic heretics.

Man who likes masturbating (a lot) seeks female physio to help with remedial work on right wrist.

FREE FAMILY PHOTOS. Sixteen-year-old wannabe photographer seeks opportunity to take pictures of your family, clothed or unclothed. Definitely sixteen and not a forty-year-old trucker, honest.

ARE YOU LOOKING FOR AN EXPERIENCED, RELIABLE STALKER? CALL TED ON

0700 13942

30. UNLIKELY TITLES FOR LOVE SONGS PART I

Side A: 3.27

You're In The Wrong Hole!

Don't Go Breaking My Ribs

If You Go Out in the Rain, Then You're a C**t

My Baby's Got the Painters In

Will you Suck My Nose?

Me and Your Mum

You're Everything That's Annoying

You're Once, Twice, Three Times a Pervert

You Look Anorexic Tonight

Do You Like it When My Dick Does That?

Fifty Whiter Shades of Pale

Lady in Bed

31. UNLIKELY THINGS TO READ IN A COOK BOOK PART I

Heston Blumenthal's 30-Minute Meals. All you need is a weapons-grade flame-thrower, two canisters of chromated copper arsenate, a state-of-the-art laboratory and a sausage.

It's an old family recipe but I didn't say it was from my family.

Test for saltiness and add semen to taste.

Throw tennis ball in air. Serve, preferably at 140 mph.

Add eight cans of lager and then you won't give a shit whether you eat this crap or not.

If you're wondering what I mean by winter veg, I mean some carrots that have been in the freezer and haven't properly thawed.

Sylvia Plath's Dinner for One. Put oven to gas mark 7, open door, place head on second shelf and lie still.

Place penis in hole. Serve.

With the cow's body hanging upside down from the kitchen ceiling you are ready to go. Next stop: *bœuf bourguignon*.

Snot is an underrated part of a balanced diet.

Drizzle the gravy onto the rabbit and then release it back into the wild.

One way to surprise and delight your dinner party is to take the apple from out of your rectum before inserting it into the pig's mouth.

If the police haven't come round by day five, they are not coming round. The body is now ready for use.

Strawberries are deadly poisonous.

Drizzle the urine on the carpet.

With this recipe, if you have not felt the need to shout 'c**t' at least five times, then you have done something very wrong.

Washing your hands after a massive dump is advisable but not compulsory.

I feel a couple of bottles of Shiraz go very well with this particular recipe, but to be honest I feel that way about literally anything I do.

At this point the rat should be dead – if it isn't, throw the mixture out and go back to the chapter entitled 'Setting the Trap'.

And, hey presto, you have now successfully scaled a fish. Time to try a mountain (this will be much harder but less fiddly).

32. UNLIKELY NAMES FOR NEW PERFUMES

MIDDLE FINGER

Cock

Infidelity

Check Your Shoes

Cheval by Findus

Coco Pops by Chanel

Speed by Huhne

Yewtree by Savile

Roy Hodgson's Whiff of Failure

Increasingly Old Spice Girls

Fromage Vieux

Give it Five Minutes

Bruce Forsyth's Old and Wrinkly

Manstink

33. UNLIKELY LINES FROM AN EROTIC NOVEL

They sat opposite each other at the table, touching hungrily. 'I think maybe I'd like a bit more sausage,' she said with a smile. 'And by that I mean your penis,' she added unnecessarily, somewhat ruining it.

Slowly but surely, he guided her into the alleyway, wedged her arse in between two wheelie bins and eased her knickers down without dropping his chips.

'You will feel pain, lots of pain, but also incredible pleasure,' he said as he watched her undress and slid her hands into the cuffs. She was curious, but couldn't help wondering if all dentists were like this.

'Show me how you pleasure yourself,' he purred. Instantly, she changed into her onesie, put on a *Downton Abbey* DVD and started eating ice cream.

The curtains billowed in the cool evening breeze, causing her silk nightdress to cling pleasingly to the enviable contours of her body and her pert, suddenly emerging nipples. Lying back on the sheets, Alphonse murmured, 'Shut the window, Brenda, it's so cold me cock looks like an acorn in a bush!'

'Oops. Sorry about that,' moaned Bartholomew as the countess elegantly undid his breeches. 'Only every time I get a boner, I shit meself.'

'I want you to lick sushi off my naked body,' she whispered.
'I don't really like fish,' he said abruptly and pissed off.

'I must apologize,' said Horatio. 'For 'tis rather small and I fear I may have become disengaged once more.'

'Fuck off, needledick,' said Princess Glenda.

She produced her handcuffs and shouted, 'I've been a bad policewoman, force yourself through my restricted entrance and call me a pleb.'

'Lick the cream off me!' she cried, her passion making her mad. 'Lick the cream off me!' she shouted louder again, but Fido was more interested in barking at the squirrel in the garden.

'All right! I'm coming!' he screamed, tired of her nagging him when he was having a shit.

He felt something stir inside him that he'd never felt before, a feeling that grew stronger and stronger as they rocked together on the bed. The joy in his head was pounding against his skull, consuming him, drowning him. It was too much to bear. And then the glorious release. The silence in the room was broken by his shouts of ecstasy: 'Come on, you Reds! One nil, get in!' he screamed.

She padded out of the bathroom in her negligee, gently closed the bathroom door and fixed him with a meaningful gaze. 'I'd give that five minutes if I were you, luv,' she purred.

'Eugh!' she screamed. 'I'm not going anywhere near that!'

'You can't put that in there,' she gasped, scarcely able to believe the size of it. 'It won't fit.' So he closed the fridge door and put the watermelon back on the shelf.

He raced into the room emitting a loud fart, and swept her into his arms before trying to give her one up the poop chute.

'Sorry, Sebastian,' she murmured. 'I would love to … you know … more than anything in the world I would … but, alas … I'm on the blob at the moment.'

He grabbed her in his arms and was consumed by her desire and her lust. Her lips found his and she pressed herself on him urgently. 'I just can't, Marion,' he said, pulling away and staring at the window. 'I had a wank half an hour ago and my balls are still really aching.'

34. BAD NAMES FOR RACEHORSES PART 3

12/1
1. STEROID LAD

17/2
6. LOUSY BLOW JOB

30/1
2. OWNED BY A C**T

93/7
7. FAT ANKLES

33/1
3. BAILIFF KNOCKING

24/1
8. CHEWY CHOPPER

200/1
4. BRIGADIER DOGFOOD

25/1
9. PISSFLAP

2/1
5. CRUEL WHIPPINGS

11/2
10. ANGRY LESBIAN

50/1

11. SENTENCED TO STONING

18/1

17. URINARY TRACT INFECTION

13/1

12. SYPHILITIC DICK

20/1

18. WHERE'S ENTWHISTLE?

4/1

13. WASTE OF FUCKING MONEY

9/2

19. ALSO RAN

99/1

14. FLOATER IN THE BOWL

16/1

20. FALL AT THE FIRST

100/1

15. DONUT BASHER

40/1

21. GOING TO GET SHOT

17/2

16. HOOK OF HAMZA

5/1

22. MASSIVE BONER

35. BAD ICE CREAM COMBOS PART 2

Luxurious

Bum & Raisin

All Natural Ingredients

100% Organic

Carrot & Quim
Cockles & Mussels
Sweaty Nuts
Meths
Vanilla Thighs
Elderflower Care Home
Rocky Marriage
Tramps of the Forest
Virgin Cherry
Banana Cream Spunk
Eggy Burp
Chunky Vomit
Mulled Wine & Priory
Brighton & Hove Albion
Velvety Chocolate Labia

36. UNLIKELY THINGS TO READ IN A SPORT AUTOBIOGRAPHY

I got to the top of the slope, I pushed off on my skis and Weeeeeeeeeeeee! all the way down to the bottom where I won a medal and stuff. Now, the next Olympics was fairly similar ...

I was remembered as one of the best players Rangers encountered ... during their season in the Irn-Bru Scottish Third Division.

I always said I didn't just want people to hear the name Oscar Pistorius and think 'Paralympian', and I'm pretty sure I've achieved that now.

It was a queer, sultry summer, the summer they electrocuted the Rosenbergs, and I didn't know what I was doing in New York, it wuz the gaffer's idea. He said to me, 'JT, why don't you and Lamps go on 'oliday for a few days before the season starts, shag a few people's birds, get your 'ead straight? Cushty.'

I always wanted a horse when I was growing up but we could never afford one, and then my dad came back from a holiday in Ireland with a brilliant racehorse. I've no idea where he got it, but he said to call it 'Shargar' and not to tell anyone about it.

Every time I dive, I try to make it better, more spectacular than my last to honour my father ... old Pa Drogba.

People always say to me, 'Audley, do you remember your fights?' And I do, literally blow by blow, it usually goes shuffle, shuffle ... shuffle, BANG. The end.

This is the story of one of the most exciting badminton matches of all time ... no, wait, hang on, come back.

'Your blood sample is giving a strange reading,' said the doctor. I felt the sweat running down that famous, tight-fitting jersey. What could this mean, here in my hour of triumph? 'It's 92 per cent alcohol, Mr "the Power" Taylor. How many pints did you have during that final?'

Rooney born in Liverpool. Rooney have brothers. Rooney play football in street. Rooney good football. Rooney sign for Everton. Score goal against Arsenal. Play England. Sign for Sir Alex man. Prostitute make Rooney do bad thing. Rooney sad.

My father always dreamed that his son would win the Tour de France, and from the day I was born in the Stanozolol and Clenbuterol Ward of the Nord Suisse Chemical Research Facility he has stopped at nothing.

'Ha ha! You pay £12.99 for this book and all the pages are blank and fall out when you open. Ha ha ha! Such is the evil genius of me, Luis Suárez …'

I'd dreamed of winning the women's shot put gold medal my whole life. Even when I was a little boy growing up in Belarus it was all I wanted to do.

I'll never forget the first time I heard that loud scream of 'Get in the hole!', as if losing my virginity wasn't difficult enough.

In the course of *Ian Bell's Great Innings*, I will be talking you through my very finest performances in an England shirt. Let's start with the best of the lot: my legendary 31 against Bangladesh in Dubai.

Of course, at school I wasn't known as 'Gazza', or even 'Paul'. My father, St John G'Ascgoyne, had been to Charterhouse too, so my housemaster, who knew him, just referred to me as 'G'Ascgoyne *fils*'.

I had always dreamed of playing rugby for England. Most Samoans do. As a boy throwing a ball around on white palm-fringed beaches, the bluest sea and the golden sun helping us run free and laugh and revel in the fun of the game, I wanted nothing more than to be at the bottom of a ruck in a quagmire in Leicester.

37. UNLIKELY THINGS TO READ IN A COOK BOOK PART 2

Use a spoon to stir the contents of the bowl and not your penis as the diagram suggests.

Put the beef in the wellington …

The duck is prepared to perfection. All that remains is to jump on it and fuck it.

Cut the onion up and then rub your hands in your cheating husband's eyes.

The best accompaniment to this recipe is a bottle of red wine, as the more pissed you are the less you will care how hard it is to do and how shit it tastes.

If you don't have whale slivers, then dolphin will probably do.

Prop the carrot upright, squat over it and then move up and down with rhythmic movements.

Whatever you do, don't panic. You can still get out of this alive.

Add lemon juice to the oyster and swallow. If you don't vomit, then eat the rest.

Place the monkey firmly in a vice, saw off its head, then season to taste.

Place the two jellies onto adjacent plates, put a cherry on top of each, carry them to the guests on a tray at chest height and shout at everyone, 'Look at my massive knockers!'

Sear the panda until brown.

Add sugar, cream and lemon, and gently rub into your partner's scrotum.

Realize you don't have the right bean from the recipe book, tip into bin, shout and scream, phone curry house.

Cooking with Faeces

If you break an egg, use some Sellotape to fix it immediately.

Add cumin to the bubbling mixture. Please check this instruction carefully because it is easy to misread with disastrous and frankly downright disgusting consequences.

If the fish is still flapping, send it back to the kitchen.

38. UNLIKELY TITLES FOR MEMOIRS PART I

I Know It Looks Bad…
by Sir Jimmy Savile

Weirdy Beardie:
The Autobiography of Mary Beard

Shagging Older Women
by Harry Styles

I'm Not on Drugs: It Is About the Bike
by Sir Bradley Wiggins

Hey, Don't Forget About Me
by Sir Chris Hoy

SAGE & Onions: The England Fast Bowler's Definitive
Take on Market Leading Accountancy and Payroll Software
by Graham Onions

I'm Not a Very Good Actor and My Girlfriend
Cheated on Me
by Robert Pattinson

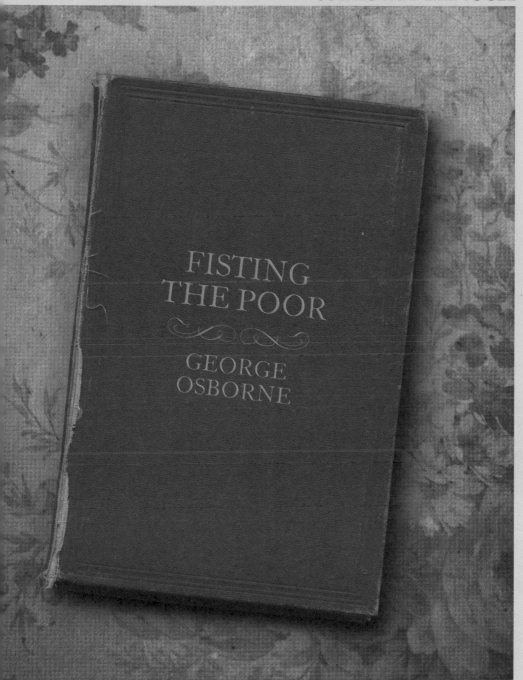

39. UNLIKELY ENTERTAINMENT LISTINGS

This Week

THE VERY BEST IN STAND-UP from a shitty room in the basement of a pub in **Camden** featuring someone who could be the next **Michael McIntyre**, a woman who is the same age as **Sarah Millican**, a bloke who looks a bit like **John Bishop** and someone who was at school with **Lee Evans**.

GALLERY BALLSAX / Exhibition of the very best in Djiboutian excrement art reconstructing some of the most powerful moments in African history using shit. *Runs until 17th.*

WANKEOKE / Soho's favourite venue combining masturbation and singing, now in its twentieth glorious year. *Phone for booth.*

NEVER ENDING STORY / The hit musical featuring the music of Limahl and Kajagoogoo. The story of Dreamer, a young boy who is Too Shy but helps take a Big Apple out of a Lion's Mouth. Tickets available from Not Very Well-Known Theatre until who knows? Fingers crossed?

SHOOBAPBEDOOPBADEDOOP / Jazz night with bands performing from all over the world. I'm sure some people would find this shit entertaining, but it beats me why. *Tickets available on door to you weirdos; £10 (concs).*

ONE MAN SHOW: STUART HALL, MY LIFE IN SHOW BUSINESS / *Postponed indefinitely.*

RED BULL SUICIDE CLUB / Back in the UK and affording an opportunity to those tired of life to die a spectacular death pretending they are trying to build a flying machine or glider. *Roof of Battersea Power Station.*

ICE DOGGING / 'Christmas is coming'. Enduringly popular event. *Somerset House ice rink from 23rd.*

TAXI-DERMY / Mobile lessons in stuffing squirrels from cabbies as they take you to your destination. Call for pick-up.

FEELING PRICED OUT OF LONDON PROPERTY MARKET? Me too. Bummer, eh?

KNOBROTTER / Horrible-sounding club night in Shoreditch playing the very best in shit-hop and new-trend 'crap'.

SICKLY DUCK TRUST / Bands, comedians and dance troupes combine for a star-studded 'bill' to raise money for ill or injured ducks. *Royal Albert Hall.*

TRUMP / Fantastic new musical utilizing the power of flatulence from the creators of *Stomp.*

FISCAL CLIFF & THE QUANTITATIVE EASERS / One of the country's top folk bands give us a rare chance to hear some of their finest originals. Support from The Bailouts.

SHITTING BRICKS / Some guy from Belgium apparently. Not sure what he does but let's hope it isn't literal ... sit at the back just in case.

CALENDAR BOYS / All-male version of the hit play starring Christopher Biggins, John McCrirrick, Colin Baker and Jasper Carrott. So far no one has come to see any of the shows. *Lyric Shaftesbury Avenue. Please come, please.*

40. UNLIKELY THINGS TO HEAR ON A SURVIVAL SHOW

'I've made a den under this tree and I'll be sleeping here for the foreseeable future. That'll teach me for banging the production secretary at the wrap party.'

'I've survived on snails, horse meat and the limbs of frogs, and I've been defecating in a hole in the ground … this French camping trip has been great.'

'Semen is, of course, a valuable source of protein. It's a long shot, guys, but worth a try.'

'To fend off dehydration we're drinking our own urine, and when that runs out, there's only American lager left.'

'The natives here use the expression *Wanapa tukata*, which means very poor Internet speed.'

'People ask me why I'm called Bear. The answer is, I keep having to shit in the woods.'

'I've skinned a chimpanzee and I've cooked and eaten the bushmeat … and sadly that means I've been kicked out of Windsor Safari Park.'

'For three hours I watched the snake, waiting for it to strike, before realizing it was a draught excluder.'

'So I've been using these leaves to wipe my bottom, which is why I've been thrown out of the salad bar.'

'No food, no water – how will they survive? Well, it's your own fault, it was you who put your parents in a care home.'

'The toughest thing to deal with is the loneliness, hour after hour, until finally, someone from your bank answers the phone.'

'Freshly cooked rabbit over an open fire – is there anything more disgusting?'

'Now I've bent this wire into a snare, and that should help me get my tea. I'll just stick it up into this vending machine and see if I can snag a Mars Bar.'

'I've spent the last three days smearing myself in fox faeces and rolling around in leaves. Those magic mushrooms were amazing.'

'Night is falling, the temperature is plummeting. Looks like I've got to huddle up against the young female researcher I specifically asked to come with me.'

'The rule with mushrooms is simple. It's ... no, is it ALWAYS eat spots, or NEVER eat spots? Oh well, these look nice ...'

'I've dug a small, deep hole to use as a toilet. I'm not worried about the animals watching me, although I'll be in trouble if the zookeeper comes in.'

'As I stare at the woman on the other side of the campsite, I've instantly made a small tent, in my trousers.'

41. UNLIKELY THINGS TO READ IN A PARENTING BOOK

When potty training, decorate an old box and keep treats in it so they know they will get a prize from the potty box whenever they use it. There is of course a danger they will just shit in the box.

Always have a roll of bubble wrap handy. Kids love it and find it very hard to get out of once you've gone round them eight times and used gaffer tape.

When taking your toddler out for a meal always carry a 'distraction bag' filled with wax crayons, books or cigarettes.

It's always great to have a comforter handy for your baby to hold on to when they need it. Ours is called Michael; he's a lovely man.

I was told that cheap nylon shorts are great for potty training. They are. In fact I wear mine everywhere, even to work.

The key is regular walks, filling meals and teaching them discipline with a stick. Oh no, sorry, that's dogs ... no, no, right first time – kids.

It doesn't matter what you do, they'll still be little fuckers from the ages of fourteen to sixteen.

If it's a girl, obviously try and give it away.

Crying at night might be a sign of hunger, so make sure your husband has a sandwich by the bed.

If the baby cries during the night, feign sleep in the hope that your partner will get up.

Give your toddler a cold bath every morning followed by a swift run. This will toughen it up for later in life when it will help run the empire.

Have as many children as possible. This is God's will. We suggest between twelve and fifteen.

When you've had enough, hand over to grandparents. Easy.

If things get too much for you, remember to take time out. Why not explore the Far East for a few years, for example?

If the child is still missing after two weeks, perhaps try calling the police.

If you have to put the baby's cot on a steep hill, try to ensure it is tethered to a tree.

Never let a baby wake you before 11 a.m. on a Sunday. They have to learn.

Babies like to experiment with words when they first learn to talk by making noises and saying things over and over again. You should discourage this by shouting, 'Shut up!' until they stop.

Grind up the sleeping pills and add to the milk; top up with whisky when required. This should assure a restful night/nights for everyone.

42. UNLIKELY LINES FROM A BOND FILM
PART 1

'Do you expect me to talk?'
'No, I was rather hoping you could suck me off.'

'This indentation in the ground is the exact spot where the Queen's parachute failed to open.'

'Put that gun away, Mr Bond – all the badgers are dead.'

'You're a beautiful girl, but is Breasty Cometobed your real name?'

'I know he won't be able to do all the stunts, but having Barry Cryer will make the puns so much better.'

'OK, Bond, I've got M and Q here, but without any vowels I can't make a word.'

'Bond, you were clearly using your mobile phone when you ran him over, so that's three points on your licence to kill.'

'Why did you untie me from the bed and rescue me from the lasers? The optician hasn't done my other eye.'

'On this laptop is the most deadly nuclear weapon ever to be placed in the hands of a secret agent. The password is … "password".'

'I want you to break into the Ecuadorean embassy and get Julian Assange out. If he's not in the first room, he'll be in the other one.'

'I did have an elaborate death planned for you, Bond, but I think I'll just shoot you now in case you escape.'

'These cutbacks have affected us badly, Bond, but nonetheless, welcome to MI4.'

'Bad news, Bond: the girl you shagged at the end of the last mission had syphilis.'

'I'm sorry, but when they called me in to see you, M, I wasn't expecting a sugar-coated peanut.'

As Bond strode into the restaurant, the maître d' caught his eye and said, 'Have you been to a Harvester before, Mr Bond?'

43. UNLIKELY THINGS TO HEAR IN A PUBLIC SWIMMING POOL

'I'm going to go to the top diving board and do something incredible: attempt to shit into a cup being held in the shallow end.'

'Oh dear, I seem to have followed through.'

'Shark!'

'Time for Aquafit. Can anyone who isn't a fat middle-aged woman please leave the pool now?'

'Has anyone lost a pair of testicles?'

'I'm doing lengths of the pool for twenty-four hours – I'm getting sponsored £10 for every verruca I accidentally swallow.'

'I don't care if it's synchronized and to music, it's still shagging!'

'Shit! Don't jump in there, you idiot. It's full of water, you might drown!'

'If you're going to carry on doing that, can you wait until that man outside has started filming?'

'What happens if you pull this big plug out?'

'Welcome to the first ever sponsored Bombing, Pissing and Heavy Petting Hour for *Children in Need*.'

'We've been oversubscribed ever since ITV aired *Splash*.'

'Are those your trunks over there?'

'Monsieur, I think you misunderstand the meaning in French of the word *piscine*.'

'Well, either it's a shark attack or that man is having a mighty strange erection.'

'Right. No one leaves until whoever did that floating poo owns up.'

'Could you swim to the pool bar and get me a cocktail?'

'Release the piranhas.'

'Oh no! Someone has dropped a black plastic brick into the pool – tell the lifeguard to go and get his pyjamas on, quickly.'

'It says don't urinate in the pool; it doesn't say anything about masturbating.'

44. UNLIKELY THINGS TO READ IN A CRIME NOVEL

The bullet was heading straight for his heart but was deflected by his cigarette case ... right into his brain.

'Who's there? ... Why don't you show yourself? ... Urrrrgh, my God, you're ugly!'

'I know you're hanging on to the window sill, but we are on the ground floor.'

'Quid pro quo, Clarice. All I know is the man you are looking for was a kids' TV presenter in the 1970s.'

'Incredible, Poirot, how did you guess?'
'Un pièce de piss, Hastings. I just hacked his voicemail and he'd left a message confessing.'

'I want to put you in some concrete overshoes. After all, it is London Fashion Week.'

The pathologist looked up from his notes. 'I've weighed the brain, the lungs and the heart,' he said, 'and you've got enough for a nice haggis. Shall I wrap it now?'

'This man is murdering people according to the seven deadly sins. Here's the plan: seeing as he's already killed five, why don't we just let him kill the other two?'

Moose Malloy had come into the Afro-American's club looking for his girlfriend Velma Valento. It was then Philip Marlowe realized he was out of his depth; he didn't have an alliterative name.

'The famous Jack Reacher?' said the tough guy in the bar. 'Sorry, but there's no way you're six foot five. I'm six one and I'm towering over you!' Reacher paused, slowly turned and stared, and said, 'Let me tell you about the life of L. Ron Hubbard ...'

Shortly after being run down and left for dead, he was sent a text reminding him he was eligible for compensation.

'It's vital these plans don't fall into the wrong hands, because ... hang on, I could swear I put them down here not two minutes ago ...'

'The timer was counting down, thirty seconds, twenty, I had to come up with something. CUPS. Four letters, not great but if I can just solve today's Countdown Conundrum I'll be in with a chance.

'This man is known to have six passports, and fourteen aliases. Yeah, this electoral roll really looks a bit dodgy.'

'They say they want a million pounds. But we only borrowed a tenner from Wonga.com last week, how can it have got that high?'

He handed over a pound of Semtex, an alarm clock and a length of detonator cord. They were the worst ingredients Ainsley Harriott had ever been given, but he bravely set about trying to make duck fajitas.

He turned the knob one way, then the other. Heard the click. The heavy door swung open revealing the valuable goods inside. Yes: the hotel minibar.

45. UNLIKELY LINES FROM A DIY MANUAL
PART 1

1. The man in the illustration wanted his house to shout a single word. Unfortunately, that word appears to be 'paedo'.

2. One way to give your living room a greater sense of space is to knock through into the neighbour's living room.

3. In a short time the dining room can be converted into a lovely sex dungeon.

4. And if you think that looks terrible, try doing *this*.

5. Defy stereotypes by using sawdust instead of carpets.

6. In our house we've massively increased the living space by getting rid of the stairs and replacing them with a sand pit.

7. No kitchen is complete without a plunge pool.

8. A glass window in the bathroom wall not only lets in light – if it's in a party wall with next door's bathroom it also allows for hours of fun.

9. One good source of chairs is a local restaurant or outdoor café.

10. We've dug a very deep basement, allowing us direct access into the Northern Line.

11. Change the atmosphere of your living space by painting all the walls black and adding whips and chains and hooks to the cornicing.

12. I can't tell you how many would-be trendsetters I have successfully talked into internal stone cladding.

13. I like to think of my house's front passage as its vagina.

14. As under-floor heating has shown us, many pipes and wires can be hidden below floorboards, as can bodies. Sorry, did I say that out loud?

15. What says cosy hospitality more than a cheery swastika in the entrance hall?

16. We wanted to give the house a 'rustic feel', so we put old car wrecks in the front garden and inbred children torturing rats in the back.

17. Walls are for wimps!

18. Throw off the shackles of convention and feel young again as you put a toilet in the middle of the lounge.

46. UNLIKELY TITLES FOR MEMOIRS PART 2

My Struggle
by David Cameron

All Got a Bit Messi
by Lionel Messi

Banking for Pets
by Harry Redknapp

A Room of One's Own:
The Julian Assange Story

Oops! I'm So Clumsy! Arrgh and Single!
There Go My Trousers…
The Miranda Hart Story

I'm Sorry I Didn't See It:
An Uneventful Look Back at Arsène Wenger's Life

Big Billy Twelvetrees Plays for England:
A Delightful New Children's Story

101 Things To Do in an Airport
by Edward Snowden

A Taste of Pickles

The Collected Musings of
Eric Pickles

47. UNLIKELY THINGS TO READ IN A DIET BOOK

Chapter 1: Don't Eat So Much
Chapter 2: Do a Bit More Exercise
The End

We're the Hairy Bikers and the secret to losing weight from our meals is to picture them being prepared by two hairy, sweaty, leathered-up northerners with grimy fingers.

Next, put the cream in the bath and roll around in it …

You Are What You Eat
Chapter 1: The Lazy, Desperate Fat Twat Baguette

Step 1: Eat what you like as often as you like
Step 2: Throw up in the toilet after each meal

The Eric Pickles Fatten Yourself Up Diet
Chapter One: Cake.

Hi, I'm 'Doctor' Gillian McKeith. You too can look like me.

This book will provide all your dietary needs for the next 365 days.
Page 1: Remove page, smear it with jam … eat

Smear the chocolate on your breasts and the inside of your thighs …

Welcome to the Shit and Water Diet

No more celery. Kill the celery vendors.

Fat people are evil.

Another way to make your partner lose weight is to cut his balls off like I did (when the voices told me to)…

Anyone who ever offers you a biscuit is worse than a playground drug pusher.

Eat a cake, go on, just one, no one's watching, just stuff it in your great big mouth, I won't tell anyone, that's good, yeah, better than a fucking salad, now touch yourself, yeah, come on, that's it, Daddy's watching you, baby, yeah.

A salad can be just as tasty as a lasagna … oh, who am I kidding? If I have to eat any more rocket I'm going to top myself.

You can eat all the carrots in the world, luv, but you'll still have a big fat arse.

Swallow enough pebbles so that you feel full.

The idea that cakes, cheese and puddings make you put on weight is an evil lie spread by UKIP.

One good alternative is to cut out solids and just drink vodka or paint stripper.

And now the moment of truth. Take off your clothes and look in the mirror. Oh my God! That's revolting! Put them back on now and get out of my fucking sight!

48. UNPLEASANT REAL ALES PART 1

GREASY COMBOVER

18 69

Bishop's Minge
Necrophilia
Doggy Poo
Old Scrotum
Nymphomaniac
Suicide Watch
Robert Robinson's
Jesus Juice
Dr Crippen's Special Ale
Putin's Polonium 210

49. BAD NAMES FOR RACEHORSES PART 4

33/1
1. NEO NAZI

5/1
6. DRUG PUSHER

2/1
2. VIOLENT SHOOTOUT

3/1
7. WHAT THE FUCK?

18/1
3. TAKEN FROM BEHIND

9/2
8. BALLS DEEP

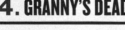
17/1
4. GRANNY'S DEAD

17/3
9. SCOTTISH TWAT

16/1
5. SHADOW ON THE LUNG

200/1
10. CAUGHT COTTAGING

201/1

11. BOTTLED IN THE FACE

 8/1

17. ASKING FOR IT

 40/1

12. RECTAL DISCHARGE

 25/1

18. VISIT THE HOOKER

 100/1

13. THAT CT FREDDY**

 6/1

19. RIBBED FOR HER PLEASURE

 99/1

14. YOUR WIFE'S A MINGER

 9/1

20. FUNDS AL-QAEDA

 300/1

15. CATCH A FALLING TURD

 13/2

21. COCK LIKE A TREE TRUNK

 7/1

16. DESECRATED GRAVE

 13/1

22. I'D GIVE THAT 10 MINUTES

50. LINES YOU WON'T HEAR IN *DR WHO* PART 2

'This plan of yours to negotiate with the Daleks isn't going to fucking work.'

'Unbelievably, he tried to fly the TARDIS into the Twin Towers, but had set it for a time before they were built, so it never happened.'

'That's the doctor all right. He went down to the docks last night and got badly beaten up again, but it's definitely him.'

'OK, Doctor, out of the TARDIS. How many have you had? Breathe into here, please.'

'Er, sorry, folks. I set the coordinates a bit wrong and we've landed in a timeless universe with no hope of getting out for billions of years. On the plus side ... '

'Doctor, I want you to take me back to the seventies, before those allegations of sexual harassment happened.'

'Oh, shit. I think a tramp has pissed in the TARDIS again.'

'Shit. If I'm not very much mistaken, I appear to have left my keys in the year 1780.'

'The doctor landed the TARDIS on the M4 and got run over by a juggernaut.'

'I've been caught speeding, Romana — you'll have to take the points.'

'I'm your new assistant, Christopher Biggins.'

'So he said, "If you think that's painful, try fucking a Cyberman ... "'

'Exterminate 99 per cent of all known household germs; exterminate 99 per cent of all known household germs ...'

'I don't care who you are, I'm nicking you for stealing a police box. We've been looking for this one since 1963.'

'And that's where I shagged Peri, over here is where Rose gave me a blow job and in here is where I banged Cleo-fucking-patra.'

'You know how the TARDIS works in terms of size and space perception? Well, my knob works along similar lines.'

'Bad news: the TARDIS came down in a volcano and that's it.'

'We can't do this. It's wrong. I love you too, but you're Dr Who and I'm a Dalek.'

'Wouldn't it be amusing if I helped Hitler win?'

51. UNLIKELY THINGS TO READ IN A CHILDREN'S BOOK PART 1

Horrid Henry stepped out of the young offenders' court and punched the air – his lawyer had got him off again.

'Well said, Great Uncle Bulgaria, if that twat carries on crying like this, he's going to flood our burrow.'

'Winnie the Pooh, if you are pretending to be a raincloud, <u>stop pissing</u>.'

It turned out it wasn't a Gruffalo trying to eat the mouse, it was Eric Pickles.

'Open Sesame,' cried Ali Baba, and the doors opened to reveal riches beyond his wildest dreams. 'Wow, finally, Bill Gates's garage.'

As the three bears came back from their 'walk' in the woods, Mummy bear told Daddy bear, 'Look, we really need an indoor toilet.'

Lord Voldemort was unimpressed with Nick Clegg's call for a reformed Upper House.

Tales of the River Bank, chapter twelve: in which all the animals are washed down the High Street into a supermarket car park.

Having spent the night with a young monkey friend,
Curious George was now BiCurious George.

Moley turned to Ratty and said, 'Did you know,
you're always within six feet of a human?'

Despite the piles of silken cushions, the
Princess complained that she could still feel the
pea underneath. 'Stop complaining – you got this
seat on Centre Court for nothing.'

'Balls, balls, bye bye, balls.' The Cat in the Hat
was neutered.

'I do not like green eggs and ham.'
  'Look, this is the train buffet, and that's what we've got.'

As Ratty ran away, Badger coughed. He was being gassed.

As the three bears returned from their walk,
they noticed that Goldilocks had put up
a sign on the door claiming squatters' rights.

And before the next morning the funny little
man had filled the room with gold.
'Ha ha ha! You'll never guess my name,'
he shrieked.
  'Yes, I will – you're George Osborne.'

52. UNLIKELY THINGS TO HEAR IN A LIBRARY

'Do you have the book of *Anal Vixens III*? I've seen the movie and wanted to see how the book compared.'

'Quick! We're under attack! Form the bookcases into a circle.'

'I said, FUCKING SHUSHHH!'

'Hello, have you got any books?'

'OK, put all the Danielle Steeles in a bag, slowly, that's it. Just do as I say and no one gets hurt.'

'There are desks available to use in the History stack or failing that you could always slip into the Popular Fiction Hot Tub.'

'Can you show me how to get that Tulisa sex video on the Internet, please?'

'So you think your puny Earth books can stop me?'

'Could you tell me which pages have the best shagging in *Fifty Shades of Grey*, please?'

'I'm Captain Hardback. Stand back, ye landlubbers, for you shall not get through. Charrggge!!'

'Four Hemingway paperbacks and a Big Mac, please.'

'Hi. Have you got any books about bomb-making, jihad or any stuff like that?'

'I am Professor Robert Langdon. We don't have much time – where is your section on cryptic codes, Jesus and shadowy cults?'

'Hello, big boy, I can read to you long and slow.'

'What were you thinking, sir? You can't just *borrow* them.'

'OK, I'm going to turn off the light and if my stamper isn't back when I turn it on again, I'll start shooting you one by one.'

'Pull over to that chair. I think you were speed reading.'

'Yes, Friday is No Underwear Day.'

'I feel so alive!'

'No, you can't just get your wife to pay the fine, Mr Huhne.'

'We're going to knock Literary Criticism through into Home and Leisure and turn this into an en-suite bathroom.'

53. UNLIKELY THINGS TO READ ON A TUBE OF TOOTHPASTE PART 2

value

toothpaste

Fresh ... arsehole fresh

✓ Quality Guaranteed

Fights gum disease, plaque and insurgency in Iraq

Now with sardine oil

Contains mind-altering drugs

Smear on testicles

Keeps your coat shiny and healthy

Burns away at your teeth while you sleep

May cause cancer

With bone-marrow gravy

Mmmm. So tasty I've come

If used daily will discolour teeth

Tested on humans

800 calories per serving

Doubles as a toilet cleaner

As used by Shane MacGowan

Serve hot

May induce flatulence

My other tube is a Colgate

Brings immediate soothing
relief to haemorrhoids

54. UNLIKELY LINES FROM A BOND FILM
PART 2

'No, I'm Pussy Galore's daughter, Loadsa Fanny.'

'Now, Bond. this looks like a perfectly ordinary ballpoint pen, because it is – we're hoping you can jab it in his eye.'

'The name's Bond. James Bond.'
 'Yes, hello, Mr Moore. I think you'll enjoy your stay at the Twilight Rest Home.'

'Here you are, Bond. Q has got you this special weapon. It's a nail gun he got from the shop he runs with his brother, B.'

'Pay attention, Bond. It looks like an ordinary mobile phone, but you can use it to send messages, surf the web and even take photos ... oh, you've got one.'

'Bond, I know you were in that helicopter with the Queen, but do you have to make love to every woman you're alone with?'

'Welcome back, Bond. Do you realize your last mission cost the country millions of pounds? I told you not to turn "data roaming" on.'

'Do you expect me to talk?'
 'No, darling, I expect you to take the speeding points and keep quiet.'

'The name's Bond. James Bond. But you can call me Jimbo.'

'Blofeld is slaughtering horses and selling them to major supermarket chains as economy beef mince.'

'It's an unusual one, Bond – the villain's lair is an old carpet warehouse in Burnley just off Junction 9 of the M65.'

'James Bond will be back in *Mission 24*. SMERSH likes this.'

'I'd like a carton of Slim Fast, shaken not stirred.'

'So, we meet at last, Mr Bond … I'm dead excited. We seemed so well matched from our emails and that!'

'The paper fell from Bond's trembling hands. It was far worse than he could have imagined … the *Mail* had published those photos of him in the Bullingdon Club with Boris and Cameron.'

'My code name is 007. My PIN is 2345 and my mother's maiden name is Johnson.'

'Bond, you've changed during your time in San Francisco.'
 'Ooh, get her! That's quite enough from you, cheeky …'

55. UNLIKELY LINES FROM A DIY MANUAL
PART 2

1. I can never look at a chimney without thinking of my boyfriend's massive cock.

2. One way to say, 'Hey! I'm a constantly changing, growing person who defies convention' is to keep scaffolding up permanently.

3. One tell-tale sign of subsidence is the house falling down.

4. A moat may suit a castle, but the effect is more difficult to achieve in a terraced house.

5. Getting planning permission is overrated in my opinion. Go with the flow, man.

6. One way to cut costs is to 'embrace cracks'. Think of your arse.

7. The house was, of course, used by a famous serial killer, but instead of hiding that fact I've decided to make a feature of it.

8. The brushed-wire effect on the paint was to give the sense of my testicles.

9. We felt the upper floor was dark, so we got rid of the roof and now the light floods in.

10. A cheap and underrated way to insulate the loft is with asbestos.

11. We were so delighted by the new look of our kitchen that I couldn't help but take my wife over the table right in front of the in-laws.

12. A basement extension not only increases the value of your home, it is also a really handy place to keep your daughter.

13. The look we were trying to achieve with this was 'crack den'.

14. Never forget: nothing in your house says more about you and who you are than your toilet-roll holder.

15. And that splash of maroon in the porch means you are ready to welcome the world with a message, and the message seems to be … 'Fuck off.'

16. Some would say that a pit in the middle of the room is pretentious, but to them I simply say, 'Vraiment?'

17. A bad smell can put off potential vendors so it's probably not great form to shit in the entrance hall.

18. If you do have to shit in the entrance hall, a great way to disguise it is to keep pigs in the living room.

56. UNLIKELY CARDS FROM A NEWSAGENT'S WINDOW PART I

HOME DENTISTRY:
CHEAP, QUICK, HYGIENIC.
CALL 'YANKER' JONES
ON 04872 112395

Baseball bat. Some bloodstains: £10. Very specific collection instructions. *Capisce?*

Fuck. Off.

Mobility Scooter: £100. (Discount if you can remove the 52-stone corpse from the seat.)

Scaffolding Pole, 2.1 metres. Make me an offer. (My name is Pavel, I've been a scaffolder for many years and, yes, I am tall.)

'Oriental style' massage. Yeah? We know what I'm saying. Evenings. Your place. Rubber sheets supplied.

Small pet carrier: £15. (P.S. He's a monkey and he's carrying the Ebola virus.)

Do you like dogs? Come and see my pictures of them. Free sweets to every caller. Contact Wilf. (The old dark house with the blue van.)

I will do anything.

Zumba ... what the fuck is it? Why does everyone keep going on about it?

Educated person needed to help me find cryptic way to write on a card that I'm after kinky sex.

This card for sale. One side unused. Open to offers.

Do you want your house to smell of farts? Worry no more.
Call me, Tarquin Windass Anderson.

Have sex with me. I'm really good. I'm also definitely a woman, not a man, even though when we meet I do have very big hands and what looks like an Adam's apple. I am all woman. Absolutely. No question.
Call Ben... Benedict.... Beniella.

57. UNLIKELY LINES FROM A FITNESS MANUAL PART I

Short, intense bursts are most effective, but enough about trying to get your shorts on …

OK, we need to work out our priorities. Are you trying to shed weight to have a better, healthier lifestyle or to make your penis look bigger?

One effective way to bring on a heart attack is …

Warming up is for sissies.

One good way to become thinner is to contract a wasting disease.

A really furious wank can burn up as many calories as a five-mile run.

The kiss of life should be administered carefully and only when someone has collapsed. (Doing it as a precautionary measure is ill advised.)

Chapter 3: Stealing Equipment from the Gym

Chapter 5: Harassing Women in the Gym

Steroids are underrated.

When I'm jogging in the park, one way to keep my mind off the burn is to steal handbags.

When working out, always put a cucumber or some other large object down your pants.

If you are watching an attractive woman work out in a mirror, never shout, 'Hubba! Hubba!'

Constipation can be your friend. If you get it really bad, each poo will not only help you shed a few pounds, but can give a really strenuous workout to your abs, chest and neck muscles.

A great way to feel that you've really made progress and have joined the long-distance running pros is to shit in the street.

Never check someone's pulse unless they want you to.

One crucial tip is that if you are standing behind a good-looking woman in an aerobics class, really try to avoid the urge to pull her tracksuit down.

58. UNPLEASANT REAL ALES PART 2

NAN'S TITS

★ FINE STRONG ALE ★

TIME FOR A CHEEKY ONE?

Don Estelle Artois

Turdburgle

Ephendrozenalene B123789

Boring Old Fart With a Beard & B.O.

Tim Brooke-Taylor

Throttled Hen

Monkeyspanker

Badger Cull

Up the Bum

Arsehole

59. UNLIKELY JOB ADS

Situations Vacant

WANKING! Now I've got your attention, have you ever considered a career in … wanking?

Why do little boys always dream of being a train driver? Because they get paid really quite well for sitting on their arses all day doing what is, let's be honest … a piece of piss.

Are you prone to complacency? Do you love the taste of alcohol? Are you addicted to adultery? Why not become an airline pilot?

Are you bored and unmotivated in your current job? Well, that doesn't bode well, does it? Don't even bother applying to us, you disloyal slob.

Fancy a job at Argos? Well, they're all in the back. Firstly, have a look through the catalogue and fill in a form.

Are you broad minded and relaxed about nudity, and comfortable with sexual matters? Why not join the Lib Dems?

Groom of the Stool – applicants wanted for this traditional post in the royal household. Andrex supplied. NB: Easier than it was in Henry VIII's day.

Management position vacant at leading London insurance firm. Apply with discretion as we haven't told the old bloke he's going yet.

Do you want to earn good money working from home 20 hours a week? You and me both, luv. Good luck.

Paper boy needed. Company bike, pension, competitive salary + bonus.

Drugs mules wanted. Ideal for people who love world travel, are good at hiding things and are relaxed about life expectancy.

Wanted! Data entry clerk. Send your CV to: A Monkey Could Do This Shit, PO Box 345, Croydon.

Mid-Staffordshire NHS: doctors wanted. Medical training an advantage but not essential.

Is there a voice inside your head telling you to chase your dreams? Then you're mad and should be sectioned.

Are you a mathematics or economics graduate? Are you good with figures? Do you understand world markets? Can you work well under pressure? Then for crying out loud, go and help George Osborne sort out his shit.

Sewage workers needed. If you're really that desperate, call us.

Enclose a copy of your CV or tweet us a pic of you in your pants.

Are you a nuclear scientist? There are loads of jobs in Iran and North Korea working on ... erm ... energy and stuff ...

Newspaper typesetters wanted. High-profile national publication is looking for new blood after forced redundancies ... the fucking twats. Contact PO Box Wank Wank Wank, Titty, Willy, Poo Jizz.

Have you given up hope of achieving your dreams? Stopped pretending you still have time to embark on that exciting career you always thought you would? Great. You're about ready to give teaching a try.

Wanted for sex offences. Man aged between 25 and 35, 5ft 7 to 5ft 9. (On second thoughts this possibly wasn't a job ad. Ed.)

Earn £70 an hour working from home. Become a prozzy.

60. UNLIKELY LETTERS TO TV STATIONS PART I

I've got an idea for the presenters of Dragon's Den. It's an enormous arse for them to shove their show up.

I really enjoyed the *Hairy Bikers* – but I feel that Delia Smith and Nigella Lawson have really let themselves go.

When you say all your programmes are HD, does that stand for 'hugely disappointing'?

Dear Sky Arts 2, I recently watched your channel and no … I'm not joking.

Dear Sky Channel 248, is that it, really?

Dear Eden, isn't it about time for some women on your channel? Yours, Adam.

Dear Channel 4, I watched your recent show *One Born Every Minute* for the full sixty minutes and was furious to note that contrary to what was promised, only two children were born, both quite close together. Please change the title to *Two Born in Any Given Hour's Time Frame* or I shall sue.

I would like to complain about the channel Alibi, otherwise known as Shit.

Dear Channel 4, I would like to complain about the grossly misleading title of your recent series *Four in a Bed*. It turned out to just be about some middle-aged couples visiting B&Bs.

I really enjoyed watching Martin Clunes visiting the islands of Britain. Is there any chance that next year ITV could pay for *my* holiday?

I'd like to complain about your show *River Cottage*. I was expecting a unique twist on *Riverdance* but featuring lots of gay men.

As a long-term resident of Newcastle-upon-Tyne, I'd like to complain about the film *War Horse* – it wasn't our house at all.

Dear BBC, I'd like to complain about the *Hairy Bikers*. I tuned in expecting to see a 1970s soft porn film about lesbians and got a cookery show.

Dear Sirs, I'd like to complain about *Embarrassing Bodies*, or *Loose Women* as you're now calling it.

Dear BBC4, thank you so much for your recent documentary about the history of string. It helped me decide which type of string to hang myself with.

Dear BBC2, why do you employ that rude Jeremy Paxman with his obnoxious style of questioning, come on, why, why? You don't know why, do you?

I've been watching *Top Gear* for twenty years now, and I'm a bit disappointed that Jeremy Clarkson still hasn't been killed in a car crash.

Dear Sky Sports, the football season has started, could you in some way try and talk up some interest in it, please?

Dear ITV, please can you explain the difference between ITV2+1 and ITV3?

61. UNLIKELY THINGS TO HEAR ON A POLITICAL DISCUSSION SHOW PART I

'The gentleman in the blue shirt – yes, you, can you move to one side so we can see the pretty girl behind you?'

'If I may, I'd like to answer that question by not saying anything at all.'

'Hang on, one of the women wants to say something …'

'Now, what are interest rates again?'

'It wasn't very well argued. I was hoping someone would come and interrupt me halfway through.'

'Let me answer that question from the attractive lady with a question of my own – would you like to go out for a drink later?'

'I'd like to ask the Syrian official – is that thing loaded?'

'In response to the man at the back – I'm sorry, if you wanted a seat at the front you should have got here earlier.'

'Question for the lady in the very short skirt in the front row. Do you know we can see everything?'

'Whatevs. ROFL. LOLS. End of.'

'I'm not being racist but …'

'Yeah? You think so? Well, why don't you just fuck off?'

'Which one of the Milibands are you again? The good one?'

'Hello, I'm the comedian who's out of their depth.'

'Anyone else getting the horn?'

'Would you like a biscuit, Mr Pickles?'

'You, the man in the tie in the third row – shouldn't you be wearing more than just a tie?'

'You, the man in the hat – shut the fuck up, you don't know what you're talking about.'

'This is boring. Can't we talk about the impracticalities of the Bercows' sex lives?'

'And we have a shorter edition of *Question Time* this week as the hall has been double booked with a badminton club.'

'Did anyone watch *Prisoners' Wives* last night?'

62. UNLIKELY TV LISTINGS

6.00 Breakfast
Bill Turnbull and Susanna Reid try to pretend the move to Salford hasn't affected the programme's guests. Featuring newspaper review by Ali from Urmston General Store, a preview of the Wigan Little Theatre pantomime and live traffic updates from the M61.

9.30 Jeremy Kyle Meets the World's Hardest Prisoners
If only.

10.00 A History of British Landscape Painting
Presented by Peter Andre.

10.30 Aung San Suu Kyi & Friends
Live from Myanmar, Burma's favourite 'It' girl presents the usual mix of music, stories and interviews. This week's guests are *Most Haunted*'s Yvette Fielding, super pianist Bobby Crush, dance troupe Diversity and Al Gore.

11.20 Ten Minute Freeview
Owing to a sackable error by someone at BBC Presentation, viewers see a teaser for *Strip Netball* from a German porn channel.

11.30 Naptime
Ninety minutes of shit about antiques, moving abroad or Dom Littlewood hassling substandard tradesmen so that old people can have a doze in front of the telly, or stay-at-home mums can put their toddlers to bed and tidy up.

1.00 Call My Bluff
Basically *Would I Lie to You* but with a bit more variation.

1.30 Call the Midwife
A couple from Chorley shout at forty-four-year-old nurse Beverley, saying she was brusque, disapproving and smelt a bit of wee.

2.00 Shit for Brains
Joe Swash presents the frankly insultingly easy daytime quiz. This week a team of lower-league footballers take on the *TOWIE* cast.

2.30 Film: Steven Seagal's Pride and Prejudice (1990)
Seagal stars as Fitz Darcy, a war veteran who returns to his family home and begins to arouse interest from the local gangsters as well as the beautiful Bennett sisters. Co-starring Pamela Anderson as Lizzie, Kelly LeBrock as Jane and Rutger Hauer as Wickham.

4.00 Who Do You Think it Is?
Members of the public join celebs to speculate on who unnamed celebrities with super-injunctions or anonymous arrests in police inquiries might be. This

week: 'Footballer AN', 'World Famous Actor' and '1970s Comedian'.

5.00 Don't Tell the Parents
Two celebrities plan a surprise for an eight-year-old boy without his mum and dad's knowledge ... oh, we really should maybe change the title.

5.30 Michael Portillo's Great Railway Journeys
Michael takes four hours to get from London to Brighton due to a broken-down train at Hassocks. He looks at an old flint wall ... for sixty minutes outside Haywards Heath and sees the inner workings of train toilets when one collapses and floods the carriage at East Croydon.

6.00 Look at These Freaks ... Awww
'Ground-breaking' Channel 4 series in which we revel in following slightly freaky-looking people but dress it up as a serious, politically correct exercise.

6.30 Man Versus Food
Audley Harrison attempts to knock the skin off a rice pudding but after twelve gruelling rounds loses on points.

7.00 An Idiot Abroad
Political documentary following Boris Johnson's trade visit to New York.

7.30 Mont Blanc: Death Mountain
Graphic documentary about the gruesome reality of mountaineering, almost certain to be pulled if some posh young Brit has a skiing accident.

8.00 Britain's Next Top Gypsy
Joe Longthorne introduces the search for a new superstar in a traveller-mad country. Judges Paddy Doherty, Cher Lloyd and David Essex assess the contenders ahead of the live final at Appleby Horse Fair.

9.00 Mr JJB
New drama series harking back to the golden age of sports casuals, price-fixed England shirts and massive golf umbrellas. Starring Patrick Stewart as Dave Whelan and Ray Winstone as Mike Ashley.

10.00 Smurgenburgenflurgendjorrgebrodds
Gripping new Scandinavian drama series set in the environmental health department of a local council office. This week Kasper becomes depressed when Birgitte buys the wrong sort of coffee for the meeting.

Bjorn Bjornosson....Soren Knut Lurkpaksen
Göran-Erik Svensson...Erik-Sven Göransson
Fjord Ikeagaard..........Stig Smorgasborden
Kasper Vikingmann.....................
................Jussi Worldsstrongestmansson
Birgitte Bjorksdottir.....Abba Volvosaabinen
Jan Molby.....................Eidur Gudjohnsen
SUBTITLES

11.00 Film: Four Funerals and an Exorcism
Richard Curtis's now-forgotten take on the *Twilight* books. Hugh Grant is stammering, well-brought-up vampire Eddy, who after being thwarted by a number of hilarious mishaps, hopes finally to be able to declare his love for new neighbour Bella (Gwyneth Paltrow). Also starring Colin Firth as Jacob the Werewolf.

63. UNLIKELY THINGS TO HEAR AT THE CIRCUS

'Roll up, roll up, can anyone give me a roll up?'

'We are a traditional circus: you don't get to see a sedated, abused elephant lumbering into a cage with a depressed, alcoholic sex offender clown at Cirque du Soleil, do you?'

'Ladies and gentlemen, please welcome the death-defying ... Bernard the Gerbil Tamer.'

'And now on *Billy Smart Late*, please welcome the very popular Wankrobats as they perform "Sex on a Trapeze".'

'Please welcome the incredible Bearded Lady who will sing her number one single "I Dreamed a Dream".'

'Please welcome the greatest lion tamer the world has ever seen: The Incredible "Stumpy" Armless.'

'And now the Moscow State Circus presents the most daring act ever ... a man openly criticizing Vladimir Putin and attempting to get away with it.'

'We'll be back after the interval, just as soon as we've doped the lions.'

'I will now attempt to do the *Times* crossword in fifteen minutes.'

'Ladies and gentlemen, please watch The Amazing Phalluso as he attempts to fasten a watch round his knob on the third hole.'

'And now death-defying zip-wire stunts from The Incredible Boris.'

'Hey presto: I'm juggling fire ... well ... three Zippo lighters.'

'Ladies and gentlemen, welcome, welcome to the incredible spectacle that is
Mal Aria's Mosquito Circus. Don't let him sting you!'

'Feast your eyes upon the assorted freaks and animals, then
remember that's what a Great Yarmouth audience looks like
and get out there and do your act.'

'People say we train them to be this obedient through cruelty and beatings,
but that's the only way these kids become good enough to trapeze in the
Shanghai Circus.'

'I haven't seen Potso the Dwarf since Jumbo came in and sat
on the chair.'

'And now the part of the show where we give a
random member of the audience the opportunity to
show us how good they are at lion taming.'

'And now the tiger will jump through the ring of
steaming piss.'

'And remember, the louder you
clap these incredible elephants, the
longer it is before we send them off
to Cash for Ivory.'

'Ladies and gentlemen, please
stand by and don your protective
clothing as we welcome the
legendary ... Excremento ...'

64. UNLIKELY VIDEO GAMES

The Leveson Inquiry (Xbox 360)

Virtua Commuter 2

Tomb Shagger

Gardeners' Question Time (Nintendo Wii)

Pub Crawl (Xbox)

Coldplay Dancercise

Jimmy Carr's Tax Avoider

Barry Scott's Cillit Bang Bang

Tulisa's Oral Star

Sonic Gets Flattened

Fruity Ninja 3, Ooh, Get Her!

Street Walker

Call of Duty XXII: Ethnic Cleanser

Lance Armstrong Blood Transfuser

The Unbearable Lightness of Being (Sega)

Angry Birds (If You Keep Playing This, Lads)

65. UNLIKELY THINGS TO READ ON A PLANE SAFETY CARD

- In the event of a landing on water … you're fucked.

- In an emergency situation adopt the brace position and feel your arse hurtling through your head.

- If the oxygen fails, put your own mask on and try to stop those around you from using theirs. It's every man for himself now, pal.

    - If something goes wrong, the people in economy can pretend to have a chance by clinging on to the seat cushion which is laughingly called a 'flotation device'. Yeah, right. Like that's gonna work.

    - If you can, try to avoid running round screaming, 'Arrghh! We're all going to die!'

    - You must refrain from smoking in the toilet unless you've had a really hot curry! Boom! Boom! Geddit?

    - Lights on the floor will guide you to the burning carcasses of the stewardesses.

- In the event of an emergency none of the stuff on this card will make the blindest bit of difference.

- Is this the card you were thinking of, sir?

- In the event of an emergency, an automatic priest will inflate to read you the last rites.

- To undo your seat belt press HERE. To undo my bra … press HERE.

- Join the dots to see what painful death awaits you.

- In the event of a water landing, get into the lifeboat and, with the axe provided, stop anyone else joining you.

- Your survival for the foreseeable future will now be in the hands of two very camp air stewards.

- If instructed, proceed to the exits and do not think about moving until you have finished your cocktail; we are not animals.

- Frequently Asked Questions: How will I find my way in the smoke? How do you inflate the lifeboat? Why are the stewardesses so orange?

- If the oxygen fails, put the mask on yourself first – you will probably find this is actually a natural reaction.

66. UNHELPFUL PLATITUDES

Good things come to those who pay the most or jump the queue.

The best revenge is to have a fulfilling life, or tape a kipper behind his radiator.

Never eat cheese.

You can lead a horse to water, but you can't turn him into lasagna.

You can fool all of the people all of the time, but why bother?

If it moves, eat it.

A fool and his buttocks are easily parted.

One swallow does not make a summer but it shows that she is into you.

You still have your health … kind of …

Diamonds are forever, but Shirley Bassey isn't.

Many hands need many arms … attached to them.

Guns don't kill people … it's the bullets coming out of them very fast, lacerating the skin, exploding bones and arteries, destroying soft tissue and vital organs, it's them that kill people. Guns only really kill if you smash them over someone's head.

Empty vessels make the most noise so make sure you wrap them in soundproof material.

There's many a shit between a fart and a bout of dysentery.

Tomorrow's another day: Wednesday, in fact.

You can be anything you want to be ... as long as it's at the fish counter in Asda Wigan.

All you have to fear is fear itself and ... your crazed, psychotic ex-husband.

You have to know your limitations, especially when you have as many as you do.

If it farts don't sniff it.

One day you'll see things differently ... unfortunately, as your eyesight is deteriorating rapidly.

There are plenty of fish in the sea ... although not as many as there were, because of quotas and overfishing.

It was just their time to go ... will you miss your testicles?

67. UNLIKELY BOOKER PRIZEWINNING TITLES PART 1

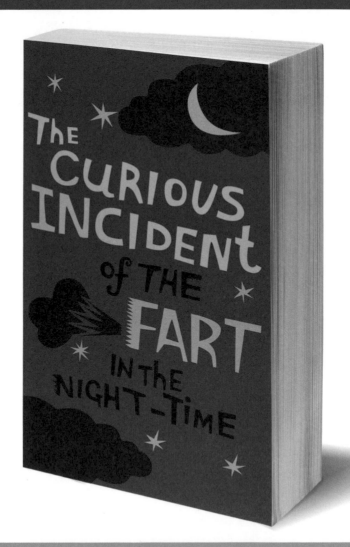

1.

*Pretentious Bollocks Set in India in a
Desperate Attempt to Win*

2.

Poo Poo Wank Piss Tits by A. S. Byatt

3.

The Satanic Nurses

4.

How to Cook with Yoghurt

5.

Alan Hansen's Great Scottish Defenders

6.

*See Spot Run. See Spot Examine His Sexuality in a
Picaresque journey through Modern Africa*

7.

Anal Vixens III

8.

What I Did on My Holidays

9.

Only When I Piss

68. UNLIKELY LINES FROM A FITNESS MANUAL PART 2

One place I really put on muscle mass was my cock.

If someone suffers a stroke or heart attack in a gym class, never point it out, as it will cause embarrassment.

Rowing machines are for the house, not for the river.

'Hi, I'm James Corden, and I'm afraid I haven't lost anywhere near as much weight as I was supposed to when I signed up to this DVD back in January, so why don't I do a funny Smithy rant at some famous friends while you do press-ups ...'

Chapter 16: Where to Have Sex in a Gym

Chapter 17: How to Hide an Erection in Lycra

Chapter 20: People Who Died in My Classes and Why

Chapter 24: How I Lost My Licence

Chapter 25: The 'Apparently' Fine Line Between 'Helping Her Stretch' and 'Groping'

Chapter 35: What to Do if You Get Your Penis Caught in the Equipment

Chapter 40: What to Do if You Shit Yourself in Your Shorts

Chapter 41: How Can Lard Be Made to Work For You?

Chapter 53: Feel the Burn as You Set the Gym on Fire

Chapter 56: Thinking of Granny to Put off Ejaculation

Chapter 57: Why I Now Realize It's Inappropriate to Enter the Women's Showers to Ask for Shampoo

Chapter 58: Exercising in Prison

Chapter 62: Avoiding Extradition

Chapter 73: Why Lance Armstrong is a Great Role Model

'By now you might already have got a real sweat on, which is a worry as you've just opened the DVD case.'

'Welcome to *Fitness Oz Style*, with me, Lisa Lycra. The exercises I'm doing aren't great, but if you keep watching all day you'll soon have wanked off about twenty pounds.'

69. UNLIKELY TITLES FOR LOVE SONGS PART 2

A
SIDE

SHE LOOKS LIKE A SNOWMAN

It's Raining Men, It's Really Shitting It Down

Throbbing Penis

I Will Always Love You (but I Still Want a Power Nap)

Touched by an Uncle

Can You Get Me Some Toilet Paper

Shit! I Thought You Were a Woman

Are You on the Blob?

Stop It. That Hurts

You Took Away My Anusol

If I Give You One, Will You Leave Me Alone?

70. UNLIKELY THINGS TO READ IN A CHILDREN'S BOOK PART 2

'During the week you'll be living with Mummy, but at weekends you'll be living with Daddy at the Crystal Temple of Scientology.'

Here is Spot. See Spot run. Run, Spot, run. That concludes the GCSE English Literature paper.

'I'm not afraid of you,' said the Gruffalo, 'you're only a little mouse,' and he stamped on him and ate him. The end.

James looked at the giant peach growing in the garden. Monsanto had really excelled themselves this time.

So that's where Spot was hiding. Now Daddy gives him a massive kick for doing that big shit on the carpet.

On Monday the very hungry Caterpillar ate a strawberry.
  On Tuesday the very hungry Caterpillar ate an apple.
  On Wednesday the very hungry Caterpillar ate a cabbage.
  On Thursday, the farmer had had enough and sprayed the very hungry caterpillar.

The wolf came up to the pigs in the house made of bricks and said, 'Do you have planning permission for this?'

Black Beauty: French translation with accompanying recipes.

'Can I come in for tea?' asked the Tiger. 'Yes,' said Lee Won, the Chinese medical practitioner.

Instead of finding the Gruffalo, the mouse came across a couple of people dogging.

'I'm not coming back to your place, Catweazle,' said the little boy. 'You're just a stinky paedo.'

'I don't care if you are the Big Friendly Giant, you'll still have to do the CRB check.'

'Children, I'm afraid we're going to have to sell the house – all because I borrowed a fiver off Wonga.com.'

Flat Stanley vowed never to chase a football across the M25 again.

'Then the Tiger drank all Daddy's beer and ate all his dinner,' explained a tired and emotional Mummy when Daddy got home.

'My name is Charlie and I have a little sister, Lola. Mummy and Daddy leave me to look after her because they are crack addicts.'

71. UNLIKELY LETTERS TO TV STATIONS PART 2

Dear *Embarrassing Bodies*, I think there might be something wrong with my penis. I've enclosed it in the envelope for you to have a look at.

Dear Channel Five, could someone please come and let us out, I think we've been forgotten about, love the *Big Brother* contestants.

Dear ITV, can you help settle an argument? I've enclosed a photo of myself – am I Ant or Dec?

Dear CBeebies, I was very disappointed by your recent episode of *In the Night Garden* when Iggle Piggle came across two men having sex in a bush.

Dear Sirs, this summer you seem to have shown nothing but sport on your channel. If this doesn't change soon I shall be cancelling my subscription to Sky Sports.

Dear Sirs, I must complain about the recent episode of *Frost*. Not only did Frost fail to solve any crimes, but at one point he was so hapless he even fell through the pub bar.

Dear Sirs, I very much enjoyed *Last Night at the Proms*, will it be on again tomorrow?

Dear Dave, I missed a programme last night, will you be showing it again?

Dear BBC, your recent documentary on child labour was excellent – please tell me where I can buy a pair of those trainers.

Dear Sirs, I'm furious. Having been told by the continuity announcer there was nudity in the following show, I sat through it for two hours before I saw any and even then it was a bloke's arse.

I watched Nigella Lawson's cookery show yesterday, and I want to make a complaint. My wife doesn't look anything like her, and her cooking's crap.

Dear E4+1, is there anywhere I can watch your selection of disappointing American sitcoms at a slightly earlier time?

Dear ITV, I'm an actress who used to be in a popular soap, I have cracking norks and would like to shower outdoors in an undersized bikini – can you help?

Dear UK Gold, I'm from the Trade Descriptions Act, please get in touch at your earliest convenience.

Dear ITV, I see that you are now broadcasting Loose Women in high definition – can you stop?

Dear BBC sports dept, is it OK if I leave my mop and bucket in here?

Dear BBC, I enjoy Bargain Hunt as much as the next man, which isn't very much, so can you please take it off air?

Dear BBC, I saw something on Antiques Roadshow that I'd like to purchase – how much is Fiona Bruce?

72. UNLIKELY BOOKER PRIZEWINNING TITLES PART 2

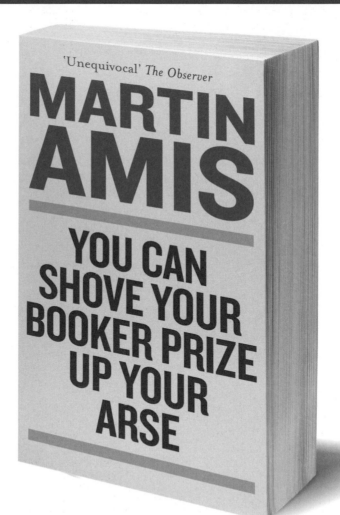

1.

Fifty Shapes of Grapes

2.

Me and My Massive Throbbing Cock

3.

The Hare with the Amber Eyes and Really Terrible Case of Myxomatosis

4.

The Girl with the Pearl Necklace

5.

Sudden Wakings by I. P. Nightly

6.

Captain Underpants and the Unbearable Lightness of Being

7.

Fisting the Hobbit

8.

The AA Book of Motorways 1978

9.

Schindler's Ark II: The Vietnam Years

73. LINES YOU WON'T HEAR IN *DR WHO* PART 3

'I've shagged all of my assistants apart from K9.'

'I'm a doctor – just pop your things off and hop up on the couch.'

'Doctor, face the truth – you're just not as good as Tom Baker.'

'I haven't had a wank for five hundred years.'

'We're going back to a time when Nick Clegg was taken seriously.'

'I'm not like other men; I've got two hearts and a massive cock.'

'They're the most highly advanced military race I've ever encountered, but don't worry, I've got a sonic screwdriver.'

'Hmm. All these cards were stuck to the wall of the TARDIS? Swedish pre-op transsexual, new in town …'

'We're about to make the jump into hyperspace … pass the Immodium.'

'You've got to believe me, Amy, it's our only chance – unzip my fly and I'll explain later.'

'The sonic screwdriver – and it plays two thousand tracks as well.'

'Hmm, we seem to have landed on a very dull planet in a not very interesting time.'

'I'm afraid the Doctor is on holiday – I'm the locum.'

'Doctor, why do you have two hearts, but only one suit?'

'It's OK, the Cybermen run on Windows XP – they'll crash any minute.'

'There's been a catastrophic tear in the space-time continuum ... but first I need a poo.'

'Let's travel forward in time an hour – that way the pizza delivery boy will have to give us a pound off.'

'Hmm, we seem to be in Cardiff again.'

74. UNLIKELY THINGS TO HEAR ON THE RADIO

'Coming up, we'll run down the top
forty former employees of this station who are now up on sex charges.'

'You're listening to the *Today* programme on Radio 4 with Vernon Kay
and Fearne Cotton.'

'And what about your fifth record, Mr Mugabe?'

'You can of course follow the chart show on our studio webcam on the
BBC website, which seems a bit pointless. It's just like watching the
shittest episode of *Top of the Pops* ever.'

'Our next caller is Mike from Telford, who I understand is not actually
a fan of any football club, he just wants to shout "c**t" really loudly …
Mike?'

'I am listening to what you're saying, Minister, but I'm also getting blown
underneath the table.'

'I'm Alan Green, it's a lovely sunny day here at Old Trafford and I'm
taking the time to think how lucky I am to be out here doing this job.'

'You're listening to *Up All Night* on 5 Live, where I'm thinking I shouldn't
have had that coffee and later I'll be worrying about my mortgage.'

'Tell us about your bloodiest stools … call now.'

'Yes, you're right, Dave from Eltham! Our Heart FM Mystery Voice was
indeed Hugh Molson, Minister of Works in the Macmillan government
between 1957 and 1959.'

'Welcome to our number one local pirate station. Coming up is a
rundown of the top ten shanties, but first it's time to win pieces of eight
with our regular daily quiz, "Walk the Plank".'

'This is 6 Music Extra, and you're listening to some phat Ibiza house with
me, Dame Vera Lynn.'

'Hello, Robbie, hello, Dave. I just had to ring up to say how good
the referee was this afternoon and how great a job our manager and
chairman are doing.'

'Welcome to *A History of Music in Six Self-Indulgent Programmes* with me,
Stuart Maconie. In episode one I'll be trying to big up someone pretentious
from the eighties while speaking in a put-on northern accent.'

75. UNLIKELY THINGS TO READ IN A BUSINESS BOOK

- Gold and other, like, precious metals and stuff are probably a better thing to invest in than, you know, gravel and manure and that.

- Don't just rob Peter to pay Paul; try and beat the shit out of Peter as well, and then go and put the frighteners on this fucking Paul character.

- The Customer Is Always a C**t.

- The retailer/customer relationship is like a marriage: cold, joyless, with both parties keeping secrets from the other.

- Remember, a man who invests £250,000 and makes a profit of £200,000 is … a jammy twat.

- If your outgoings are more than five times your earnings, then you are a moron.

- Many people advocate extensive research and a well-thought-out plan before setting up a business, but I think that's bollocks. Just look at your horoscopes and see if you have Venus rising.

- If all the logical options have been exhausted and you are still making a loss, why not try selling a loved one for sex?

- The most important thing to have in business is a lot of cheese.

- All humans are disgusting, naïve twats who are there for you to cheat, dupe and steal from.

- If you're not spending a million pounds on pointless flashy luxuries then you're doing something wrong.

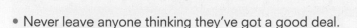

- Never leave anyone thinking they've got a good deal.

- Here's an idea. Try finding a commodity that people want and buy it all up. That way, when they want some of it, you can sell it expensively and make a large profit. Simple, really.

- Great business plans are like bars of gold: if you see one, steal it.

- Bear in mind that if interest rates are 2 per cent over base and you had to borrow at least 50 per cent on your office mortgage … oh, fuck this, I wanted to be a poet. I had promise. I won a bloody prize in sixth form and everything. I put up with the ridicule from the rugby team, the captain of whom actually turned out to be gay and took my virginity on the last day of school in the long grass at the back of the cricket pavilion, after which I've been to therapy week in week out for the last ten years, which is why I have to write this mindnumbing shite to pay for it and why I don't have time to commit to a relationship and make something of my life. What is the fucking point? Well? What is it? Goodbye, cruel world … arrgghh!

76. UNLIKELY CARDS FROM A NEWSAGENT'S WINDOW PART 2

YOUR FACE IN THIS WINDOW. IF YOU AREN'T FUCKING CAREFUL. YEAH?

Catch herpes the fun way! Call Steve.

Do you have a horse you no longer want? I will give it a good home ... for a bit ... call Pete's Burger Emporium.

My name is Tim, I am slim.
I spend my time obsessing with rhyme.
I look for one who likes some fun
And when we're there, the laughs we'll share.
(P.S. Please don't have a short fuse and beat me up like my previous partners.)

Jeffrey Dean Glaziers. Smash window and take card for free estimate.

Slag. Up for anything. 20p. (People who think teeth are important need not apply.)

Genuine licensed buttock reader. Have your fortune told. Only women though.

Do you smell? If so, find out what of. Call Bill.

Horrifying psychotic pervert seeks same to share the cost of a cadaver. Must have GSOH

Have you seen that film *The Sessions*? Can you come and do that for me? I'll pay, I'm not disabled or anything, just really ugly and unpleasant.

Lovely Amish guy seeks pure woman for company and only a teeny bit more.

Sophisticated erudite polymath with esoteric, some might say rather fin de siècle tastes, seeks woman with massive tits.

Looking for woman to help me sort out a penis reduction. Yeah, you heard me, baby ... it's ... oh, who am I trying to kid? You can't see it in all the folds of flab, like a drawing pin in a rolled-up mattress. I tell myself it's normal but it can't be, please be my friend, bring a shotgun.

Suck my knob or die wondering.

77. UNLIKELY THINGS TO HEAR ON A POLITICAL DISCUSSION SHOW PART 2

'Welcome to *This Week*. My first question is to Michael Portillo – did you ever shag Peter Lilley?'

'You … yes, you … yes, you, there … you, the man pointing at me … oh, sorry, it's my reflection.'

'On *Question Time* we ask: is politics still taken seriously on television? First question from the man in the red nose on the unicycle.'

'No, with all due respect, you've had your say, now shut the fuck up.'

'And the question for the man at the end there, in the shirt, the tie … no, next to him … Nick Clegg! That's it.'

'So, is politics being dumbed down? Jedward, what do you think?'

'Welcome to *This Week*, and in tonight's painfully over-extended simile we'll be likening my hair to the euro. It's disappearing, but does anybody really care?'

'Tonight we ask: how close is the coalition? With me is David Cameron, and Nick Clegg is in our Shetland studio.'

'The next question is for Ed Miliband and it's from Gromit – and he wants to know, what time will you be in for your tea?'

'Welcome to *Question Time*. The first question comes from me, and it is: why are these halls getting smaller and smaller?'

'Tonight we have 150 people on the panel, and just five in the audience. I can't help feeling someone's misread the seating plan.'

'Nick Clegg, you have to speak on the fifty-pence tax rate for one minute without hesitation, deviation, repetition or bursting into tears over the mess you've made of your career.'

'Welcome to *Young Persons' Question Time*. An audience of 200 people … will be watching this on television.'

'Hello, I'm Andrew Neil with the answers to all the big questions. Firstly, yes, it is a wig.'

'Next week on *Question Time* we'll be talking about the budget cuts. If you'd like to be in the audience, it'll be coming from my front room.'

'Question from the man in the back in the janitor's uniform … yes, we will be finished soon, you can lock up then.'